The Ethical Dimensions of Global Development

Institute for Philosophy and Public Policy Studies
General Editor: Verna V. Gehring

About the Series. This new series grows out of a collaboration between the Institute for Philosophy and Public Policy at the University of Maryland and Rowman & Littlefield Publishers. Each slim volume in the series offers an insightful, accessible collection of essays on a current topic of real public concern, and which lies at the intersection of philosophy and public policy. As such, these books are ideal resources for students and lay readers, while at the same time making a distinctive contribution to the broader scholarly discourse.

About the Institute. Established in 1976 at the University of Maryland and now part of the School of Public Affairs, the Institute for Philosophy and Public Policy was founded to conduct research into the conceptual and normative questions underlying public policy formation. This research is conducted cooperatively by philosophers, policy makers and analysts, and other experts both within and outside of government. The Institute publishes the journal *Philosophy & Public Policy Quarterly* and the series Institute for Philosophy and Public Policy Studies with Rowman & Littlefield Publishers.

War after September 11

Genetic Prospects: Essays on Biotechnology, Ethics, and Public Policy

The Internet in Public Life

Community Matters: Challenges to Civic Engagement in the 21st Century

The Ethical Dimensions of Global Development

The Ethical Dimensions of Global Development

EDITED BY
VERNA V. GEHRING

ROWMAN & LITTLEFIELD PUBLISHERS, INC.
Lanham • Boulder • New York • Toronto • Plymouth, UK

ROWMAN & LITTLEFIELD PUBLISHERS, INC.

Published in the United States of America
by Rowman & Littlefield Publishers, Inc.
A wholly owned subsidiary of The Rowman & Littlefield Publishing Group, Inc.
4501 Forbes Boulevard, Suite 200, Lanham, Maryland 20706
www.rowmanlittlefield.com

Estover Road, Plymouth PL6 7PY, United Kingdom

British Library Cataloguing in Publication Information Available

Library of Congress Cataloging-in-Publication Data
The ethical dimensions of global development / edited by Verna V. Gehring
    p.   cm.
  Includes bibliographical references and index.
  Contents: The ethical dimensions of global development: an introduction / William A.
Galston—Looking backward to look forward: reckoning with past wrongs—Retribution
and reconciliation / David A. Crocker—Complicity in mass violence / Stephen L.
Esquith—Tolerating the intolerable: the case of female genital mutilation / Xiaorong
Li—Child labor abroad / Roland Pierik—Development ethics and globalization / David
A. Crocker—Globalization and its discontents / Herman E. Daly—Globalization's major
inconsistencies / Herman E. Daly.
  ISBN-13: 978-07425-4961-6 (alk. paper)
  ISBN-10: 0-7425-4961-5 (alk. paper)
  ISBN-13: 978-0-7425-4962-3 (pbk. : alk. paper)
  ISBN-10: 0-7425-4962-3 (pbk. : alk. paper)
  1. Globalization—Moral and ethical aspects. I. Gehring, Verna V.
JZ1318.E865 2006
174—dc22   2006050968

Printed in the United States of America

♾™ The paper used in this publication meets the minimum requirements of American
National Standard for Information Sciences—Permanence of Paper for Printed Library
Materials, ANSI/NISO Z39.48-1992.

Contents

Contents

III: The Effects of Globalization

Preface

The essays in this work first appeared as articles in *Philosophy & Public Policy Quarterly*, the journal sponsored by the Institute for Philosophy and Public Policy at the School of Public Policy, University of Maryland. William A. Galston, former director of the Institute for Philosophy and Public Policy, contributed the introduction, and research scholars David A. Crocker and Xiaorong Li also contributed several chapters. The volume has benefited from the conversation and thought of all of the research scholars at the Institute for Philosophy and Public Policy: David A. Crocker, Robert K. Fullinwider, Peter Levine, Xiaorong Li, Judith Lichtenberg, Mark Sagoff, Jerome M. Segal, Robert Wachbroit, and David Wasserman. The editor is grateful for all of their helpful comments and thoughtful advice in the development of this volume. Many thanks also go to Carroll Linkins and Richard Chapman for their help and kindness in bringing the essays to press.

Verna V. Gehring
Editor
Institute for Philosophy and Public Policy
School of Public Policy, University of Maryland
College Park, Maryland

The Ethical Dimensions of Global Development: An Introduction

William A. Galston

Globalization is more often invoked than defined, a fact that makes it difficult to discuss the relationship between globalization and anything else with even tolerable precision. So let me begin by attempting a definition. As a broad concept, "globalization" denotes the declining significance of national boundaries, while specific conceptions single out different dimensions—such as the flow of goods, people, information, technology, or ideas—along which this decline is alleged to occur. Note that increasing flows by themselves do not suffice to prove that globalization is taking place. It is conceivable, for example, that nations in full control of their borders may decide to admit more immigrants or guest workers. The deeper meaning of globalization is the proposition that nation-states are losing the power to control what occurs within their borders and that what transpires across (or without regard to) borders is rising in relative significance.

Some argue for a kind of determinism. Modern technology, they suggest, makes it impossible for national governments to control the flow of information, which in turn inexorably pushes closed regimes to open up and to liberalize. As recent events show, matters are more complicated than this. Employing technological countermeasures collectively dubbed "The Great Firewall of China," the leaders of the People's Republic have successfully blocked access to websites deemed subversive. We can say with confidence, however, that

absent such policies, today's technology permits the near-instanta-
neous transfer of information without regard to distance. A few
decades ago, Muslim protests over Danish cartoons mocking the
Prophet Muhammad might have remained confined to a single small
country. Now, protesters in Copenhagen, Lahore, and Jakarta can
simultaneously view identical images and coordinate their strategies
while everyone else can observe and discuss what the aggrieved
group is doing.

Development and Its Challenges

Some features of the current landscape stand out. Compared to thirty
or forty years ago, international trade represents a larger share of the
world's economic output. The flow of capital, investment, and technology has increased even more rapidly. Whether seeking opportunity or fleeing danger, significant numbers of Asians, Africans, Latin
Americans, and Muslims from the Middle East have taken up resi-
dence in the nations of Europe and North America. The result: to a
greater extent than in the years immediately following the Second
World War, citizens of advanced industrialized nations are living
cheek by jowl with immigrants from unfamiliar cultures practicing
minority religions. Diversity is more than a contested concept; for
hundreds of millions of people, it is a new and often unwelcome fact
of life.

These and parallel developments have raised new issues for policymakers, many of which are discussed in this volume. Nations with
large new populations cannot avoid taking a stand on controversial
practices: the law must permit, forbid, or regulate female genital
mutilation and a host of other practices. They must decide which rituals fall within the protected zone of religious exercise and the extent
to which religious adherents can manifest their faith in public places.
Development and its challenges raise numerous questions. Among
several of many issues raised in this volume are:

**Can general ethical principles be brought to bear on questions
of globalization?** The globalization of public attention forces governments and citizens to consider the ethical dimensions of other nations'
conduct and to reflect on their responsibility for events far beyond
their border. Former president Bill Clinton has said that his worst mistake was not intervening to prevent or halt the genocide in Rwanda,
despite the lack of connection between that horrible event and US

national interests as traditionally defined. US legislation and diplomacy helped create the context in which the apartheid regime in South Africa concluded that it had little choice but to release Nelson Mandela and surrender power to a black-majority government. To what extent do Americans now have the right to pass judgment on the strategy that the new government employed to promote stability and reconciliation? David A. Crocker suggests that we can bring general philosophical principles concerning the nature of punishment and the good society to bear critically on Archbishop Desmond Tutu's strategy of maximizing social harmony. For his part, Stephen Esquith explores the other side of the transnational coin, when governments act to bring about, not justice and reconciliation elsewhere in the world, but rather starvation and mass violence. When are democratic citizens "complicit" in such acts, and through what means can they be educated to recognize the complex links between their daily lives and terrible events thousands of miles away?

Do economic development and self-government require a duty of care? Applying general moral principles to specific cases requires more attention to particular circumstances than most proponents of global standards are willing to give. In the course of considering the issue of child labor, Roland Pierik points out that not all nations share the same conception of childhood and that common definitions of harmful work are often overly broad. Worst of all, well-intentioned efforts to improve the well-being of children can backfire. It is easy for policymakers in wealthy countries to believe that if they can shut off markets for goods made with child labor, children will leave looms, brickyards, and factories and go to school. In the real world, terminating their employment can leave them worse off than before. Because wealthy nations have an impact on their poorer trading partners, they cannot avoid some responsibility for the consequences of their policies. Further, as Xiaorong Li points out, tensions arise when certain cultural and religious traditions clash and practices undermine the protection of basic liberties and rights. Perhaps a political version of the Hippocratic oath—First, do no harm—would be an appropriate guide. More broadly, responsibility for consequences suggests a duty of care, what lawyers would call due diligence on the part of governments to consider the pragmatic as well as principled dimension of policy and to avoid policies that may well be popular (because they appeal to widely held public principles) but in specific cases do more harm than good. These strictures apply, not only to efforts to promote economic development in other countries, but also to progress toward political goods such as democratic self-government.

Is economic destiny crucial to individual autonomy? The globalization of ethical attention has implications for governance. Scholars such as Martha Nussbaum and Peter Singer argue that the most defensible moral stance is strongly cosmopolitan and that we are not entitled to apply an ethical discount rate to the well-being of human beings with whom we have no ties of family, ethnicity, nationality, or citizenship. Others counter that lowering or erasing particularist political ties is unwarranted and unwise. Herman E. Daly distinguishes between cosmopolitan globalization and internationalization—a community of real national communities. He argues in favor of the latter model: effective national boundaries will not only prevent a race to the economic bottom but also give democratic publics a better chance of retaining control over their own destiny. On this view, it is not immoral for citizens who share in political institutions and have a common destiny to distinguish between themselves and other human beings: while we are not entitled to harm those who live beyond our borders, we do not have the same affirmative responsibility to promote their well-being as we do for fellow citizens.

One suspects that the dialogue between particularism and cosmopolitanism will continue through the century on which we are now embarked. Over time, perhaps, an emerging agreement on the content of global human rights will help define the boundary between what we owe to others as human beings and what we may rightly do as citizens of specific communities. In the meantime, democratic governments will face a series of difficult choices, at home and abroad, without a clear moral compass. We can expect a steady stream of sins of omission and commission as nations fumble toward a conception of transnational responsibility than can gain and sustain public support.

Retribution and Reconciliation

David A. Crocker

In his recent book, *No Future without Forgiveness*, Archbishop Desmond Tutu evaluates the successes and failures of the South African Truth and Reconciliation Commission (TRC). The chair of the TRC, Tutu defends the Commission's granting of amnesty to wrongdoers who revealed the truth about their pasts, and he lauds those victims who forgave their abusers. While recognizing that a country must reckon with its past evils rather than adopt "national amnesia," Tutu nevertheless rejects what he calls the "Nuremberg trial paradigm." He believes that victims should not press charges against those who violated their rights, and the state should not make the accused "run the gauntlet of the normal judicial process" and impose punishment on those found guilty.

Tutu offers practical and moral arguments against applying the Nuremberg precedent to South Africa. On the practical side, he expresses the familiar view that if trials were the only means of reckoning with past wrongs, then proponents of apartheid would have thwarted efforts to negotiate a transition to democratic rule. The South African court system, moreover, biased as it was toward apartheid, would hardly have reached just verdicts and sentences. Tutu points out that trials are inordinately expensive, time consuming, and labor intensive—diverting valuable resources from such tasks as poverty alleviation and educational reform. In the words of legal theorist

Martha Minow, prosecution is "slow, partial, and narrow." Rejecting punishment, Tutu favors the TRC's approach in which rights violators publicly confess the truth while their victims respond with forgiveness. Powerful practical reasons may explain the decision to spare oppressors from trials and criminal sanctions. But, as I shall show, no *moral* argument—at least neither of the two that Tutu provides—justifies rejection of the Nuremberg paradigm.

The Argument against Vengeance

In the first of these moral arguments, the argument against vengeance, Tutu offers three premises for the conclusion that—at least during South Africa's transition—legal punishment of those who violate human rights is morally wrong. He asserts: (1) punishment is retribution, (2) retribution is vengeance, and (3) vengeance is morally wrong.

Although Tutu understands that forgiveness may be appropriate for any injury, at one point he claims that amnesty provides only a *temporary* way for South Africa to reckon with past wrongs. He provides no criteria, however, to determine at what point punishment for crimes should be reinstated, and he also offers no reasons that punishment is justified in normal times. Further, one might wonder on what grounds Tutu would deny exoneration for those who committed human rights violations *after* the fall of apartheid and who now wish to exchange full disclosure of their wrongdoing for amnesty.

Is Punishment Retribution?

Consider the first of Tutu's three premises in his argument against punishment. While Tutu assumes that punishment is no more than retribution, he fails to define what he understands by "punishment." He does not, for example, explicitly identify legal punishment as state-administered and intentional infliction of suffering or deprivation on wrongdoers. Tutu also says almost nothing about the nature and aims of legal punishment. He fails to distinguish court-mandated punishment from therapeutic treatment and social shaming, among other societal responses to criminal conduct. Tutu does not consider the various roles that punishment may play—such as to control or denounce crime, isolate the dangerous, rehabilitate perpetrators, or give them their just deserts—and whether these roles justify the criminal sanction. He does at one point say that the "chief goal" of "retributive justice" is "to be punitive." Tutu apparently takes it as a given that "punishment" means "retribution" and that the nature of legal punishment is retributive.

Tutu does at times concede that trials have two other aims, at least during South Africa's transition: vindicating the rights of victims and generating truth about the past. Again and again, Tutu states that victims of past wrongs have the right—at least a constitutional right and perhaps also a moral one—to press criminal charges against and seek restitution from those who abused them. He also extols the "magnanimity" of individuals who, like former South African president Nelson Mandela, have not exercised this right but are willing to forgive and seek harmony (*ubuntu*) with their oppressors. These statements suggest that Tutu regards legal punishment not merely as a means to retribution but also as a way to affirm and promote the rights of victims.

Tutu also endorses the credible threat of punishment as a social tool to encourage perpetrators to tell the truth about their wrongdoing. The TRC did not grant a blanket amnesty to human rights violators or pardon all those convicted of rights abuses committed during apartheid. Instead the TRC offered amnesty to *individual* perpetrators *only if* (1) their disclosures were complete and accurate, (2) their violations were politically motivated, and (3) their acts of wrongdoing were proportional to the ends violators hoped to achieve. According to Tutu, individuals who fail to fulfill any of the three conditions have a strong incentive to apply for amnesty and reveal the whole truth. It is precisely because violators are threatened with trial and eventual punishment that they realize that making no application for amnesty or lying about their wrongdoing is too risky. Without such a threat of trial and punishment, the TRC is unlikely to have had the number of perpetrators who did come forward to confess gross wrongdoing.

But Tutu cannot have it both ways. He cannot both reject actual punishment and still defend the threat of punishment as efficacious in dispelling lies and generating truth. Hence, Tutu's acceptance of a "threat to punish" practically commits him to a nonretributive and consequentialist role for punishment, since without occasionally making good on the threat to punish, such a threat loses credibility.

Tutu does not bring enough precision to the term "retribution." He seems, at points, simply to identify retribution with legal punishment. Instead, one must understand retribution as one important *rationale* or *justification* for and a constraint upon punishment.

Proponents of the retributive theory of punishment offer a variety of competing accounts, but all agree that any retributive theory minimally requires that punishment must be "backward looking in important respects." That is, justice requires that a crime is punishable as, in the words of lawyer and legal theorist Lawrence Crocker, "a matter of the criminal act, not the future consequences of conviction and punishment." These future consequences might comprise such good things as deterrence of crime, rehabilitation of criminals, or promotion of reconciliation. For the proponent of retributivism, however, the infliction of suffering or harm, something normally prohibited, is justified because of—and in proportion to—what the criminal has done antecedently. Only those found guilty should be punished, and their punishment should fit (but be no more than) their crime.

Some supporters of the retributive theory of punishment assert, moreover, that only (and perhaps all) wrongdoers deserve punishment, and the amount or kind of punishment they deserve must fit the wrong done. Harvard philosopher Robert Nozick explains desert in terms of both the degree of wrongness of the act and the criminal's degree of responsibility for it. Retribution as a justification for punishment requires that wrongdoers should get no more than (and perhaps no less than) their "just desserts."

Is Retribution Vengeance?

The second premise in Tutu's argument against punishment—that retribution is (nothing but) vengeance or revenge—is flawed as well. Given Nozick's understanding of retribution as "punishment inflicted as deserved for a past wrong," is Tutu right to treat retribution and revenge or vengeance as equivalent? Both retribution and revenge share, as Nozick puts it, "a common structure." They inflict harm or deprivation for a reason. Retribution and vengeance harm those who in some sense have it coming to them. Following Nozick's brief but suggestive analysis, I propose that there are at least six ways in which retribution differs from revenge.

Retribution addresses a wrong. First, as Nozick observes, "retribution is done for a wrong, while revenge may be done for an injury or slight and need not be done for a wrong." I interpret Nozick to mean retribution metes out punishment for a crime or other wrongdoing while revenge may be exacted for what is merely a slight, an unintended injury, an innocent gaze, or shaming in front of one's friends.

Retribution is constrained. Second, Nozick also correctly sees that in retribution there exists some internal upper limit to punishment while revenge is essentially unlimited. Lawrence Crocker concurs: "an absolutely central feature of criminal justice" is to place on each offense "an upper limit on the severity of just punishment." This limitation "is the soul of retributive justice." It is morally repugnant to punish the reluctant foot soldier as severely as the architects, chief implementers, or "middle management" of atrocities. Retribution provides both a sword to punish wrongdoers and a shield to protect them from more punishment than they deserve. In contrast to punishment, revenge is wild, insatiable, unlimited. After killing his victims, an agent of revenge may mutilate them and incinerate their houses. As Nozick observes, if the avenger does restrain himself, it is done for external reasons having nothing to do with the rights or dignity of his victims. His rampage may cease, for instance, because he tires, runs out of victims, or intends to exact further vengeance the next day.

Notably, Martha Minow and others subscribe to a different view. Minow suggests that retribution is a *kind* of vengeance, but curbed by the intervention of neutral parties and bound by the rights of individuals and the principles of proportionality. Seen in this light, in retribution vengeful retaliation is tamed, balanced, and recast. It is now a justifiable, public response that stems from the admirable self-respect that resents injury by others.

While Minow's view deserves serious consideration, Nozick, I think, gives us a picture of vengeance—and its fundamental difference from retribution—that better matches our experience. Precisely *because* the agent of revenge is insatiable, limited neither by prudence nor by what the wrongdoer deserves, revenge is not something admirable that goes wrong. The person seeking revenge thirsts for injury that knows no (internal) bounds, has no principles to limit penalties. Retribution, by contrast, seeks not to tame vengeance but to excise it altogether. Retribution insists that the response not be greater than the offense; vengeance insists that it be no less and if possible more. Minow attempts to navigate "between vengeance and forgiveness," but she does so in a way that makes too many concessions to vengeance. She fails to see unequivocally that retribution has essential limits. Vengeance has no place in the courtroom or, in fact, in any venue, public or private.

Retribution is impersonal. Third, vengeance is personal in the sense that the avenger retaliates for something done antecedently to her or her group. In contrast, as Nozick notes, "the agent of retribution need have no special or personal tie to the victim of the wrong for which he exacts retribution." Retribution demands impartiality and rejects personal bias while partiality and personal animus motivate the thirst for revenge.

The figure of Justice blindfolded (so as to remove any prejudicial relation to the perpetrator or victim) embodies the commonplace that justice requires impartiality. Justice is blind—that is, impartial—in the sense that she cannot distinguish between people on the basis of familiarity or personal ties. This not to say, however, that justice is impersonal in the sense that she neglects to consider an individual's traits or conduct relevant to the case. Oddly, Tutu suggests that the impartiality or neutrality of the state detracts from its ability to deal with the crimes of apartheid. He defends the TRC because it is able to take personal factors into account. He writes:

> One might go on to say that perhaps justice fails to be done only if the concept we entertain of justice is retributive justice, whose chief goal is to be punitive, so that the wronged party is really the state, something impersonal, which has little consideration for the real victims and almost none for the perpetrator.

Although justice eliminates bias from judicial proceedings, it may be fair only if it takes certain personal factors into account. Because Tutu confuses the impersonality or neutrality of the law with an indifference to the personal or unique aspects of a case, Tutu insists that judicial processes and penalties give little regard to "real victims" or their oppressors.

Retribution takes no satisfaction. A fourth distinction between retribution and revenge concerns the emotional tone that accompanies—or the feelings that motivate—the infliction of harm. Agents of revenge, claims Nozick, get pleasure, or we might say "satisfaction," from their victim's suffering. Agents of retribution may either have no emotional response at all or take "pleasure at justice being done." (Adding to Nozick's account and drawing on the work of political theorists Jeffrie Murphy and Jean Hampton, I should add that a "thirst for justice" may—but need not—arise from moral outrage over and hatred of wrongdoing.)

Retribution is principled. Fifth, Nozick claims that what he calls "generality" is essential to retribution but may be absent from revenge. By this term, Nozick means that agents of retribution who inflict deserved punishment for a wrong are "committed to (the existence of some) general principles (prima facie) mandating punishment in other similar circumstances."

Retribution rejects collective guilt. Nozick, I believe, helpfully captures the main contrasts between retribution and revenge. To these, I add a sixth distinction. Mere *membership* in an opposing or offending group may be the occasion of revenge, but not of retribution. Retributive justice differs from vengeance, in other words, because it extends only to individuals and not to the groups to which they belong. In response to a real or perceived injury, members of one ethnic group might, for instance, take revenge on members of another ethnic group. However, the state or international criminal court could properly mete out retribution only to those individuals found guilty of rights abuses, not to all members of the offending ethnic group. Since collective guilt has no place in an understanding of retributive justice, revenge and retribution should not be conceived as equivalent. Tutu makes precisely this mistake.

Following the Hegelian dictum "first distinguish, then unite," Nozick promptly concedes, as he should, that vengeance and retribution can come together in various ways. Particular judicial and penal institutions may combine elements of retribution and of revenge. The Nuremberg trials, arguably, were retributive in finding guilty and punishing some Nazi leaders, punishing some more than others, and acquitting those whom it found not guilty as charged. But Tutu is right to say that the Nuremberg precedent was contaminated, compromised by revenge or "victor's justice." As he notes, Nuremberg used exclusively allied judges and failed to put any allied officers in the dock. However, Tutu neglects to affirm the achievements of Nuremberg: it vindicated the notion of individual responsibility for crimes against humanity and defeated the excuse that one was "merely following orders." One reason that Nuremberg is an ambiguous legacy is that it had both good (retributive) and bad (vengeful) elements. In no case can one accept Tutu's second premise that retribution is *nothing but* vengeance.

What of Tutu's third premise that vengeance is morally wrong? When I shift the focus from vengeance to the agent of revenge, I accept Tutu's premise. Unlike the agent of retribution, the agent of revenge does wrong, or at least he is morally blameworthy. He retaliates and inflicts an injury without regard to what the person impartially deserves. If the penalty *happens* to fit the crime, it is by luck; the agent of revenge is still blameworthy since he gave no consideration to desert, impartiality, or generality. If, as is more likely given the limitless nature of revenge, the penalty is more excessive than the crime, the agent of revenge is not only culpable but also his act is morally wrong. Nonetheless, Tutu's overall argument against vengeance is unsound since two of its premises are not acceptable.

The Reconciliation Argument

Tutu proposes a second moral argument against the "Nuremberg trial paradigm" for South Africa's transition and others like it. Tutu rejects retributive justice on the grounds that it prevents or impedes reconciliation. He understands reconciliation as "restorative justice," the highest if not the only goal in South Africa's reckoning with past wrongs. Tutu defends amnesty and forgiveness as the best means to promote reconciliation. What does Tutu mean by the vague and not infrequently contested term "reconciliation" and its synonym "restorative justice"? Tutu explicitly defines restorative justice (in contrast to retributive justice) as reconciliation of broken relationships between perpetrators and victims:

> We contend that there is another kind of justice, restorative justice, which was characteristic of traditional African jurisprudence. Here the central concern is not retribution or punishment. In the spirit of *ubuntu*, the central concern is the healing of breaches, the redressing of imbalances, the restoration of broken relationships, a seeking to rehabilitate both the victim and the perpetrator, who should be given the opportunity to be reintegrated into the community that he has injured by his offense.

Although Tutu in this passage uncharacteristically leaves room for punishment, he understands the "central concern" of restorative justice as the reconciliation of the wrongdoer with his victim and with the society he has injured. The wrongdoing has "ruptured" earlier relationships or failed to realize the ideal of *ubuntu*. *Ubuntu*, a term from the Ngunui group of languages, refers to a kind of social harmony in which people are friendly, hospitable, magnanimous, compassionate, open, and nonenvious. Although Tutu recognizes the difficulty of translating the concept, it seems to combine the Western ideal of mutual beneficence, the disposition to be kind to others, with the ideal of community solidarity.

Tutu regards social harmony or communal harmony as the *summum bonum*, or highest good. He concedes that South Africa must in some way "balance" a plurality of important values—"justice, accountability, stability, peace, and reconciliation." Whatever "subverts" or corrodes social harmony, however, "is to be avoided like the plague." Presumably, whatever maximizes social harmony is morally commendable and even obligatory.

Tutu may believe that *ubuntu* presents so lofty an ideal that no one would question its justification or importance. In any case, he offers little argument for its significance or supremacy. He does seek to support it by calling attention to its African origins. He also remarks that, while altruistic, *ubuntu* is also "the best form of self-interest," for each individual benefits when the community benefits.

As it stands, neither defense is persuasive. The moral disvalue of apartheid, also a South African concept, has nothing to do with its origins. Similarly, the geographical origin of *ubuntu* does not ensure its reasonableness. Further, although individuals often benefit from harmonious community relationships, the community also at times demands excessive sacrifices from individuals. Moreover, dissent or moral outrage may be justified even though it disrupts friendliness and social harmony.

Tutu offers practical objections—as well as moral ones—to seeking retributive justice against former oppressors. He does not consider the practicability of *ubuntu*, however, as a goal of social policy. He does not discuss, for example, what to do with those whose hearts cannot be purged of resentment or vengeance. Nor does he explain how society can test citizens for purity of mind and heart—how it can determine who has succeeded and who has failed to assist society toward this supreme good.

Tutu's concept of reconciliation can be compared to two other versions of social cooperation: (1) nonlethal coexistence and (2) democratic reciprocity. In the first, reconciliation occurs just in case former enemies no longer kill each other or routinely violate each other's basic rights. This thin sense of reconciliation, attained when cease fires, peace accords, and negotiated settlements begin to take hold, can be a momentous achievement. Reconciliation as nonlethal coexistence demands significantly less and is easier to realize than Tutu's much thicker ideal that requires friendliness and forgiveness. Societies rarely, if ever, choose between harmony and mere toleration. Historically, societies have to choose between toleration among contending groups and the war of each against all. A more demanding interpretation of reconciliation—but one still significantly less robust than Tutu advocates—is democratic reciprocity. In this conception, former enemies or former perpetrators, victims, and bystanders are reconciled insofar as they respect each other as fellow citizens. Further, all parties play a role in deliberations concerning the past, present, and future of their country. A still-divided society will surely find this ideal of democratic reciprocity difficult enough to attain— although much easier than an ideal defined by mutual compassion and the *requirement* of forgiveness. Some would argue, for instance, that there are unforgivable crimes or point out that a government should not insist on or even encourage forgiveness, since forgiveness is a matter for *victims* to decide.

Not only is Tutu's ideal of social harmony impractical, but it is also problematic because of the way it conceives the relation between the individual and the group. Tutu's formulation of *ubuntu* either threatens the autonomy of each member or unrealistically assumes that each and every individual benefits from the achievements of a larger group. Sometimes individuals do benefit from social solidarity. But life together is often one in which genuinely good things, such as communal harmony and individual freedom, my gain and your gain, conflict. In these cases, fair public deliberation and democratic decision making are the best means to resolve differences. A process that allows all sides to be heard—and encourages all arguments to be judged on their merits—respects public well-being, individual freedom, and a plurality of values.

This analysis of alternative conceptions of reconciliation not only shows that Tutu's ideal is unrealistic but also that it pays insufficient attention to individual freedom, including the freedom to withhold forgiveness. In making social harmony the supreme good, Tutu unfortunately subordinates—without argument—other important values, such as truth, compensation, democracy, and individual accountability. In some contexts, social harmony—if it respects personal freedom and democratic deliberation—should have priority. In other contexts, society may pursue other equally important values, for example, justice, which might require a society to indict, try, sentence, and punish individuals who violated human rights. If social harmony is judged to have priority over other values, that judgment should emerge not from a cultural, theological, or philosophical theory but from the deliberation and democratic determination of citizens.

This chapter appeared previously in *Report from the Institute for Philosophy & Public Policy,* vol. 20, no. 1 (Winter/Spring 2000).

Sources

Desmond M. Tutu, *No Future without Forgiveness* (Doubleday, 1999); Martha Minow, *Between Vengeance and Forgiveness: Facing History after Genocide and Mass Violence* (Beacon Press, 1998); David A. Crocker, "Civil Society and Transitional Justice," in *Civil Society, Democracy, and Civic Renewal,* edited by Robert K. Fullinwider (Rowman & Littlefield, 1999); David A. Crocker, "Reckoning with Past Wrongs: A Normative Framework," *Ethics & International Affairs,* vol. 13 (1999); David A. Crocker, "Truth Commissions, Transitional Justice, and Civil Society," in *Truth v. Justice: The Morality of Truth Commissions,* edited by Robert I. Rotberg and Dennis Thompson (Princeton University Press, 2000); Paul van Zyl, "Evaluating Justice and Reconciliation Efforts," *Perspectives on Ethics & International Affairs,* vol. 1 (1999); Lawrence Crocker, "The Upper Limits of Punishment," *Emory Law Journal,* vol. 41 (1992); Geoffrey Cupit, *Justice as Fittingness* (Clarendon Press, 1996); Aryeh Neier, *War Crimes: Brutality, Genocide, Terror, and the Struggle for Justice* (Times Books, 1998); Robert Nozick, "Retributive Punishment," in *Philosophical Explanations* (Belknap Press, 1981); Bill Berkeley, "Aftermath: Genocide, the Pursuit of Justice and the Future of Africa," *Washington Post Magazine* (October 11, 1998); Jean Hampton, "The Retributive Idea," and Jean Hampton and Jeffrie G. Murphy, "Hatred: A Qualified Defense," both of which appear in *Forgiveness and Mercy,* edited by Jeffrie G. Murphy and Jean Hampton (Cambridge University Press, 1988); Steve Coll, "Peace without Justice: A Journey to the Wounded Heart of Africa," *Washington Post Magazine* (January 9, 2000); James Bohman, *Public Deliberation: Pluralism, Complexity, and Democracy* (MIT Press, 1996); Amy Gutmann and Dennis Thompson, *Democracy and Disagreement* (Harvard University Press, 1996).

From:

The Ethical Dimensions of
Global Development

ed. Verna V. Gehring
(Rowman & Littlefield, 2007)

Complicity in Mass Violence

Stephen L. Esquith

In 2003 the Food and Agriculture Organization of the United Nations concluded that "Overall, the number of undernourished people in the countries in transition grew from 25 to 34 million between 1993–1995 and 1999–2001." The concept of "transition" has come to mean many things during this period. Recently we have witnessed the expansion of the European Union from fifteen to twenty-five countries, the tenth anniversary of the first democratic elections in South Africa, the tenth anniversary of the Rwandan genocide, and the intensification of the war in Iraq. Fifteen years after the euphoria of 1989, it is unclear in what direction "countries in transition" are moving, or even who is "in transition" and who is not. It is clear that what is occurring in "countries in transition" cannot be separated from the larger processes of globalization and that "transition" covers a much wider range of countries than was thought when the Berlin wall fell.

In this context, I want to discuss the question of responsibility for mass violence and its relationship to democratic citizenship. The conventional wisdom is that responsibility for mass violence comes in two forms: moral and juridical. Moral responsibility is less stringent in the sense that so long as coming to the aid of those in need is not too risky, then regardless of who is at fault, moral persons have a duty of beneficence to intervene and help. If it is too risky for them, regardless of who is at fault, they are not bound to act on this duty. In contrast, juridical responsibility depends upon who is at fault, and in cases of mass violence those who have contributed causally, either through their actions or omissions, ought to be held legally liable. Juridical responsibility is a matter of justice, not a matter of moral beneficence, and failure to meet this responsibility is punishable by law.

One finds attempts to fill in the space between these two forms of responsibility with a general notion of political responsibility. Citizens in, for example, a democratic society bear more political responsibility for the violent acts of their government than do subjects of a tyranny. But, many forms of mass violence are not the acts of governments, let alone democratically elected governments. What responsibility, if any, do democratic citizens have for mass violence when it occurs through complex international, multinational, and other global institutions? How are we to map the responsibilities of democratic citizens in a world in which one finds many types of democracy and in which our conventional intuitions about moral and juridical responsibility are at best insufficient?

I suggest that we use two related ideas, complicity and reenactment, to make better sense of the responsibilities of democratic citizens in the current context. Complicity refers to a wide range of responsibilities between moral responsibility on one side and legal liability on the other. Reenactment refers to a particular form of democratic political education that enables citizens to recognize their constitutive roles in the generation of political power and the imposition of mass violence. Asking "complicity" to do this much work is itself risky. The term comes to us with strong connotations. Relying on reenactments is no less dangerous; reenactments can just as easily provide vicarious and cathartic experiences as they can prompt greater clarity and civic engagement.

Having said this, however, it still seems possible to articulate how certain kinds of reenactments can encourage appropriate feelings and beliefs about responsibility for mass violence among democratic citizens. As Martha Nussbaum has noted, this was the Greek playwright Euripides' purpose in *The Trojan Women*. At a time when Athenian democracy was committing mass violence on the island of Melos, Euripides found a way to reenact that massacre through a play about the aftermath of the Trojan War. Similarly, contemporary playwrights often return to classical themes in order to bring to life the issue of responsibility for mass violence. Peter Sellars's production of *The*

Children of Herakles aspired to be a similar vehicle for political education after the events of September 11, 2001. Reenactment is a particular kind of democratic political education that can make better use of the notions of complicity in an age of escalating violence and deepening poverty across national borders. To be effective as democratic political education, reenactments must prompt democratic deliberation, not substitute catharsis and polemic for it.

My goals are (1) to explore the relationship between complicity and responsibility, (2) to understand why moral sympathy is an inadequate virtue for democratic citizens, and (3) to suggest how re-enactment as a form of democratic political education can clarify and motivate political responsibilities.

Complicity

Determining who is an accomplice to a crime, after or before the fact, is never easy. Distinguishing between collaborating with an occupy-ing force and sharing some responsibility for the consequences of occupation short of criminal guilt is equally, if not more, difficult. So much is left to chance that settling accounts can become arbitrary. Yet, the urge to identify and punish complicity, not in round numbers but down to the decimal point, is hard to resist.

This is only part of the problem. The report of the South African Truth and Reconciliation Commission (TRC) identified institutional, not just individual, accomplices after the fact, including religious denominations and parts of the legal profession. Beyond that, the report criticized the Commission itself for focusing on exceptional perpetrators while ignoring the "little perpetrator" in each of us: "It is only by recognizing the potential for evil in each one of us that we can take full responsibility for ensuring that such evil will never be repeated."

If talk of complicity in crimes against humanity may only produce frustration and hyperbole, why raise the issue of complicity in global poverty? The lines of causation are even *more* intricately woven, sug-gesting to many that only duties of beneficence based upon moral sympathy can possibly exist for mass violence. Before addressing the inadequacy of moral sympathy as a response to global poverty and mass violence, let me note an important assumption about the connections between poverty and violence in the argument that I am about to make.

I assume that there is an unhappy, close relationship between war, on the one hand, in the form of civil wars, militia terrorism, and wars of aggression, and deprivation, in the form of poverty, hunger, and famine on the other. Some attempts to reduce global poverty have actually exacerbated mass violence, and unless the political causes of mass violence are addressed, global economic development programs will fail. In this chapter I will refer to deprivation and war together as mass violence, leaving aside the very complicated question of how they influence each other in particular cases.

Responsibility

What can be done to sharpen the sense of responsibility of citizens who are committed to democracy, and benefit from global economic development, but at the same time fail to recognize their own complicity in the global structures of power that generate unprecedented levels of mass violence?

Commonly, we think of responsibilities of beneficence or justice as the responsibility that an individual has for his or her actions. In this case, responsibility depends upon the freedom of the individual to make and act on his or her decisions. Varying degrees of freedom lead to varying degrees of responsibility. One must also consider responsibility to others to remedy existing conditions, or to compensate for past wrongs and ill-gotten gains. It is in discussions of responsibilities to others that the vexed question of collective responsibility for the causes of and benefits from the exercise of power, as well as the effects of mass violence, arises.

Collective responsibility requires less a *philosophical* investigation into the notion of free will than it requires a *political* investigation into the fabric of democratic citizenship, which is why there is a need for the concept of complicity as a type of political responsibility not reducible to individual moral guilt or legal liability. Complicity in this sense is a symptom of compromised democratic citizenship, that is, alienation from the democratic political process. In this sense, victims, perpetrators, and bystanders share an important characteristic: for complex and different reasons they all find themselves outside the democratic political process. This kind of damage to the body politic can only be repaired through democratic political education.

Democracy

Consider the practice of democracy—not the classical or the modern ideal, but actually existing democracy, what Thucydides attempted to describe in ancient Greece and what Tocqueville thought he saw in nineteenth-century America. The practice of democracy today is not the constitutional rules of the road for individual citizens of nation-states. It is a network of intersecting and overlapping structures of power, including multinational corporations, multi-lateral organizations, international nongovernmental organizations, social movements, and (but not centered on) nation-states. It is this complex network that defines how we use the democratic language of citizenship, participation, and membership. Like the ancient Athenian assembly, today's global institutions and movements determine how we *practice* democracy. They are the engines of power that drive actually existing democracies, and they are what the contemporary distinction between transitional and consolidated democracies attempts to capture. This theoretical attempt is failing, but that is no reason to abandon the notion of democratic transition. On the contrary, properly understood, the notion of democratic transition can help us restore the fabric of democratic citizenship in practice. At a time when self-described consolidated democracies have lost the qualities of a participatory and deliberative democratic political culture that have been thought to distinguish them from merely transitional democracies, a more inclusive notion of democratic transition can provide the ground for more extensive bonds of political responsibility.

Over the past half century many post-colonial and post-authoritarian societies in Latin America and Africa, then in Eastern Europe and the area covered by the former Soviet Union, have moved erratically toward democracy. By comparison, liberal democratic societies initially prided themselves on their records of successive electoral regime changes, stable democratic culture, and sustained economic growth, in other words, democratic consolidation. It has been politically expedient for politicians and intellectuals seeking a justification for the distortions caused by the half century of Cold War mobilization to make invidious comparisons between their own consolidated democracies and the travails of barely transitional new democracies. They have done this without recognizing how closely linked are consolidation and transition. Without the support of client states, mercenaries, guest workers, and illegal and unfair terms of trade, consolidated states would not have been able to maintain their relative stability.

However, as the Cold War era gave way to a new period of warfare, mixing hi-tech spectacles, cruel ethnic campaigns by local militias and warlords, and conventional territorial warfare, it has become much more difficult to ignore the relationship between consolidation and transition. It has become clearer that consolidation, understood as political stability and economic growth for some, often has been purchased at the expense of violent instability and deprivation for others. One sees this in disputes about import quotas and crop subsidies, not just in the pitched battles between client states and mercenaries on one side and insurgents on the other.

Grudgingly, citizens of self-proclaimed consolidated democracies have grasped the transitional nature of their own democratic projects. Sometimes this recognition has taken the form of monetary reparations paid to living survivors or their families by the state and corporations complicit in past crimes against humanity (or guilty of less serious violations of human rights). For example, in 1999 the German government, in cooperation with the United States, arranged to limit reparations to survivors of slave labor from corporations that collaborated with the Nazi regime. More frequently, reparation has been symbolic. For example, some universities have opened their books to allow for discussion of the involvement of their founding fathers in slavery, and some municipalities have begun to require that private contractors disclose any ties to the history of slavery before they can be employed on public projects.

Further evidence of the need to expand our working concept of democracy is the way that the related distinction between nationals and foreigners and the distinction between nearby and distant strangers are failing us. Democracy, whether we call it transitional or consolidated, has also been associated with territory on which fellow citizens enjoy commonly-understood conceptions of justice. The patterns of migration, remittance, and illicit trafficking in arms, drugs, and human beings that have made national boundaries so porous have not just increased the speed and range of international trade and war. As philosopher Eduardo Mendieta describes, what is "now" is not always what is "here," what is "here" is sometimes distant yet familiar; sometimes nearby, routine and still unfamiliar. One thing that this compression of time and space has done is forced citizens in democratic societies to reexamine the familiar notion of sympathy. It has become hard to distinguish between the stranger in our midst to whom even limited sympathy is owed, and the distant foreigner with whom we have more contact than our most intimate compatriots.

Sympathy

As these changing circumstances have put pressure on the boundaries of democratic citizenship, the task of democratic political education has changed as well. Citizens can no longer simply be taught to abide by the rule of law, participate in periodic elections, and be prepared to play the role of the loyal opposition. Such liberal democratic virtues were designed for idealized self-sufficient nation-states. Unable to separate clearly transitional and consolidated democracies, and unable to distinguish between distant and nearby strangers, citizens committed to democracy now need a more practical democratic political education. If they are to act responsibly in the unavoidable transitions continually faced by democratic societies, citizens must learn how to recognize the constitutive roles they already play in a complex global network of power and violence.

How can democratic citizens find enough footing to recognize their complicity in this complex network? Some have argued that the answer to these questions may depend upon restoration of the moral sentiment of sympathy, not an easy task. Philosopher Jonathan Glover, for example, argues that any sympathy for the victims of mass violence is today likely to be eroded by (1) the vast physical distance that separates victims and perpetrators, (2) the seemingly "clean" and "smart" technologies that are used to impose violence, (3) the precedents that already exist for relying on mass violence in political conflicts, and (4) the slippery slope that leads to the escalation and spread of mass violence. Only if we can find a way to restore our moral imagination, that is, our capacity to recognize the shared humanity that unites victims and perpetrators, are perpetrators or bystanders likely to feel much sympathy for victims. Even a realistic political scientist such as Robert O. Keohane seems unable to resist the lure of sympathy, or what he calls "transnational bonds of empathy":

> Our principal task as scholars and citizens who believe in more accountability is to build support within our powerful, rich countries for acceptance of more effective and legitimate multilateral governance to achieve human purposes, for stronger transnational bonds of empathy, and for the increased external accountability that is likely to follow.

Glover's chronicle of the erosion of moral sympathy, unfortunately, leaves us wondering how such "bonds of empathy" possibly can arise. The moral intuitions we normally rely upon to guide our actions toward the world's poor are indeed in disarray. Similarly, our moral intuitions about what counts as a crime against humanity are equally flawed. Instead of seeing these crimes as products of corrupt state power and the militia groups this corruption spawns, we remain mesmerized by the immorality of individual perpetrators and bystanders. Our moral principles are in no better shape than our intuitions. The principles that have been offered to reorder our moral intuitions are either too stern or too idealized. Political philosopher Thomas Pogge, for example, scolds us for being "hunger's willing executioners," suggesting a parallel between blind consumerism and collaboration with Nazi war crimes. Ethicist Onora O'Neill rightly rejects John Rawls's principles of justice because they rest upon an idealization of the self-sufficient nation-state and its basic institutions while ignoring the way that transnational institutions actually shape our desires and needs.

In theory, the Rawlsian method of reflective equilibrium—that is, the movement back and forth between moral intuitions and institutional principles in order to get a better fit between the two—seems like a plausible approach to the problem of philosophical justification. However, so long as our intuitions remain in such disarray and the principles to which we are most wedded are out of step with transitional and global circumstances, we will need something more to prompt our imagination than reflective equilibrium. We must find a way to move back and forth between the competing points of view of those O'Neill calls "impoverished providers" and the complicity of bystanders to—as well as perpetrators of—mass violence. This is not a purely reflective process. It requires forms of embodied participation in the overlapping worlds of unfamiliar neighbors and distant strangers. Describing exactly what this might look like is not easy, but at least for students and faculty it would include civic engagement projects, community service-learning programs, and study abroad programs that were part of an integrated curriculum, and not isolated experiences.

The needed moral imagination, then, will not take the form of sympathy (or "empathy") for, in Rawls's words, "the least advantaged class." Compelling images of the starving poor and the innocent victims of violence may prompt vague feelings of guilt and sympathy, but the results of this sympathetic reaction in the current context are often perverse. Consider journalist Philip Gourevitch's admittedly outraged assessment of the United Nations refugee camps built in Zaire for refugees of the 1994 genocide by members of Hutu Power in Rwanda:

> This was one of the great mysteries of the war about the genocide: how, time and again, international sympathy placed itself at the ready service of Hutu Power's lies. It was bewildering enough that the UN border camps should be allowed to constitute a rump genocidal state, with an army that was regularly observed to be receiving large shipments of arms and recruiting young men by the thousands for the next extermination campaign. And it was heartbreaking that the vast majority of the million and a half people in those camps were evidently at no risk of being jailed, much less killed, in Rwanda, but that the propaganda and brute force of the Hutu Power apparatus was effectively holding them hostage as human shields. Yet what made the camps almost unbearable to visit was the spectacle of hundreds of international humanitarians being openly exploited as caterers to what was probably the single largest society of fugitive criminal against humanity ever assembled.

Sympathy under these conditions may not be even a necessary condition, let alone a sufficient one, for appreciating the networks of transitional and global violence that link the victims of Hutu Power with, Gourevitch goes on to say, "all of us who paid taxes in countries that paid the UNHCR" (The United Nations' High Commissioner for Human Rights). If recognizing complicity requires that we place ourselves squarely within this shifting frame of reference, we actually may have to make an effort to resist feelings of sympathy for the dramatic images of starving and suffering refugees. Such feelings only may reassure us that we have not lost our capacity for sympathy. We also will have to find a democratic practice through which more fine-grained distinctions regarding complicity can be made. Holding all taxpayers accountable is no better than holding no taxpayers accountable.

Reenactment

Democratic citizens in the current context have a better chance of learning to recognize their complicity in the exercise of power and the creation of mass violence through a process of deliberation and discussion prompted by reenactment than through the cathartic evoca-

tion of moral sympathies. By reenacting our imperfect ways of politically coming to terms with global power and local violence, we may
be able to see ourselves within this complex picture, instead of uncrit-
ically identifying with victims or observing them more comfortably
from afar. Tribunals and commissions are necessary for this process,
but alone they are not enough. As development ethicist David A.
Crocker has argued, when war crimes tribunals, truth commissions,
and other political proceedings are reexamined under a critical light,
citizens are better able to see the limitations of legal punishment and
moral forgiveness. Actively engaged as an audience to the reenactment
of these spectacles, philosopher Hannah Arendt argued, citizens can
begin to form political judgments in particular cases. It is in this sense
that reenactments may enable citizens to move with poise and humil-
ity between their familiar surroundings and the worlds of impoverished providers and bystanders. These reenactments most often take
the form of films and dramatic performances, but they can also be
sculpture, poetry, and fiction. What they have in common is the goal
of prompting a critical understanding of the complicity that links the
"impoverished providers," bystanders and perpetrators who have
appeared before tribunals and commissions seeking justice, understanding, and sympathy.

Schematically, reenactment is a public performance that creates a
temporary space in which to contest official efforts to counter mass
violence. Within this space, one finds the opportunity for critical self-
reflection on the relationship between complicity and other types of
responsibility.

Reenactments, such as the work of the filmmaker Mandy
Jacobson (*Calling the Ghosts; The Arusha Tapes*) and the artist William
Kentridge (*History of the Main Complaint; Ubu and the Truth
Commission*), create a space in which viewers, listeners, and readers
can see themselves among the sufferers and benefiting bystanders of
mass violence without losing sight of differences in degree as well as
kind between actual sufferers and beneficiaries who regret this suffering.

William Kentridge's *Ubu and the Truth Commission*, performed in
1997 in collaboration with Jane Taylor and the Handspring Puppet
Company, is particularly instructive because of its approach to understanding the goals of democratic political education in an age of mass
violence. Despite its serious limitations, South Africa's Truth and
Reconciliation Commission (TRC), like other truth commissions and

war crimes tribunals, has created an almost unprecedented opportunity for democratic political education. What distinguishes the TRC and these official institutions from reenactments such as *Ubu and the Truth Commission* is the way that the latter frame questions of responsibility and raise questions about the evolution of power in a manner that encourages democratic imagination and practice rather than cynicism, apathy, or moral relief.

Kentridge is perhaps best known for his animated film studies of the responsibilities of beneficiaries of apartheid, most notably *The History of the Main Complaint* (1996). The medical examination of the white tycoon Soho Eckstein takes us inside Soho and back through his entanglement in the violence of apartheid. Soho's diagnosis is performed in the protected space of a hospital room, with Soho surrounded by a wall of sympathetic doctors. However, in a coma Soho is haunted by his own complicity with apartheid as he "drives" back in time. Nobel laureate writer J. M. Coetzee describes the action in Soho's dream this way:

> A third drive sequence begins. Soho passes by a body lying at the roadside. He passes a roadside fight in which two men attack a third, kicking and beating him brutally (the sequence looks forward to the appalling torture sequences in the 1997 theatre production, *Ubu and the Truth Commission,* with their strong debt to cartoon violence). The points of impact on the victim's skull are marked with red crosses. The skull is superimposed over Soho's, his too, in an X-ray, is revealed to be marked. A whole field of crosses appears on the windscreen, and is wiped away. An eye blinks, with the same effect. In the space of the screen, created by Eisensteinian montage, windscreen and eye and monitor become metonymically the same.

It is this internalized violence that torments Soho and that takes center stage in *Ubu and the Truth Commission*. The challenge, Kentridge suggests, is to render the proceedings of the TRC so that this violence is neither obscured and forgotten nor harmlessly preserved in memory.

Ubu and the Truth Commission consists of Kentridge's animated drawings projected on a screen at the back of a stage on which actors, puppets, and puppeteers reenact testimony before the TRC and the accompanying dramas that surrounded the official hearings. According to Kentridge, there is a great, unavoidable irony in the TRC's efforts to come to terms with mass violence. He notes that as "people give more and more evidence of the things they have done they get closer and closer to amnesty and it gets more and more intolerable that these people should be given amnesty." Democratic citizens after mass violence must learn to interpret and live with this irony. The more effective the TRC is in providing a relatively peaceful public forum for the private stories of victims and perpetrators, the more it denies this irony and the more unacceptable it is as a method for resolving the disputes over intentions and responsibilities that it has opened up. *Ubu* is designed to contest the peaceful closure some advocates of the TRC hoped to achieve, but in a way that advances the process of political dialogue.

The casting and imagery in *Ubu* captures this irony without declawing it. The movements and expressions of the long-suffering puppets who testify before the TRC are much more human than the human figures, Ma and Pa Ubu, who venomously battle to see who will shred the records and who will use them to buy amnesty. It is this juxtaposition, Kentridge observes, upon which the success of the re-enactment turns.

> But the question of how to do justice to the stories bedevils all of us trying to work in this terrain. With *Ubu and the Truth Commission* the task is to get a balance between the burlesque of Ubu and Ma Ubu and the quietness of the witnesses. When the play is working at its best, Ubu does not hold back. He tries to colonize the stage and be the sole focus of the audience. And then it is the task of the actors and manipulators of the puppets to wrest that attention back. This battle is extremely delicate. If pushed too hard the danger is that the witnesses become strident, pathetic, self-pitying. If they retreat, they are swamped by Ubu. But sometimes, in a good performance and with a willing audience, we make the witness' stories clearly heard and throw them into a wider set of questions that Ubu engenders around them.

In the end Pa Ubu sacrifices the three-headed dog puppet that represents the secret police and other "dogs of war" in order to finagle his amnesty. He and Ma Ubu sail off into the setting sun animated on the back screen—a sun that is also an open eye that may see them for what they are. We cannot be sure. This tentative promise of a future day of reckoning suggests that the TRC is only the beginning of the story, not the final chapter on apartheid. "This theatre," Kentridge writes,

> rekindles each day the questions of the moment. How to deal with a guilt for the past, a memory of it. It awakes every day the conflict between the desire for retribution and a need for some sort of social reconciliation. Even those people (and there are a lot) who will have nothing to do with the Commission and who are in denial of the

truths it is revealing are, in their very strident refusals, joining in the debate.

Admittedly, this is still an optimistic view of the prospects for democratic discourse. Cultural reenactments like *Ubu and the Truth Commission* remind us, in director Jane Taylor's words, that the TRC is a "monumental process, the consequences of which will take years to unravel." The significance of cultural reenactments like *Ubu and the Truth Commission* is that political education conveys a sense of unavoidable indeterminacy. In Kentridge's own words,

> To say that one needs art, or politics, that incorporate ambiguity and contradiction is not to say that one then stops recognizing and condemning things as evil. However, it might stop one being so utterly convinced of the certainty of one's own solutions. There needs to be a strong understanding of fallibility and how the very act of certainty or authoritativeness can bring disasters.

Films like *Calling the Ghosts*, which traces the subsequent political odyssey of women who were victims of genocidal rape at Omarska, and productions like *Ubu and the Truth Commission* are encouraging signs that our democratic imagination has not entirely failed us in these most difficult times. Such cultural reenactments provide a language that citizens can use to come to terms with the complexity of political responsibilities. They also create a space within which citizens can learn how to adapt this language to their own particular circumstances.

Cultural reenactment must be done in local dialects but in such a way that protects the cosmopolitan promise of democracy, even if it can never be fully realized. Kentridge reports this response of one audience member after a performance of *Ubu and the Truth Commission*.

> And after a performance of *Ubu and the Truth Commission* a woman came up to us, obviously moved by what she had seen. She said she was from Romania. We expressed surprise that the play had been accessible to her as it was so local in its content. "That's it," she said. "It is so local. So Local. This play is about Romania."

Ubu is no more about Romania than *The Trojan Women* or *The Children of Herakles* is about September 11, 2001. However, just as adaptations of ancient plays can provide an open-textured language for political resistance and a means for affirming democratic principles of justice, cultural reenactments of war crimes tribunals and truth commissions can broaden the meaning of complicity and responsibility so that these terms carry across national boundaries. Their audiences do not fall into the trap of acknowledging the suffering of others only to bring attention to their own capacity for sympathy. Rather than act as judges of guilt, innocence, or sincerity, with the aid of re-enactments, they may become self-critical participants in a dialogue over what they are responsible for beyond the reach of legal indictment and outside the realm of moral forgiveness. By rephrasing the indictments of war crimes tribunals and the amnesties of truth commissions, reenactments can become vehicles for democratic political education. That is, they are ways of orienting citizens through various forms of democratic participation toward the power and violence for which they are responsible.

This chapter appeared previously in *Philosophy & Public Policy Quarterly*, vol. 24, no. 4 (Fall 2004).

Sources

Thomas Carothers, "The End of the Transition Paradigm," *Journal of Democracy*, vol. 13, no. 1 (2002); for a discussion of the responsibility of democratic citizens for mass violence when it occurs through complex international, multinational, and other global institutions, see Thomas Pogge, *World Poverty and Human Rights* (Cambridge, MA: Polity, 2002); Martha C. Nussbaum, "Compassion & Terror," *Daedalus* (Winter 2003); the quote concerning the "little perpetrator" in each of us occurs in Mark Sanders, *Complicities: The Intellectual and Apartheid* (Durham, NC and London: Duke UP, 2002); for a discussion of the political causes of famine, see Alex de Waal, *Familie Crimes: Politics & the Disaster Relief Industry in Africa* (Bloomington, IN: Indiana UP, 1998); for a discussion of the escalation of mass violence in the twentieth century, see Charles Tilly, *The Politics of Collective Violence* (New York: Cambridge UP, 2003); on aspects of democratic consolidation, see Juan J. Linz and Alfred Stepan, *Problems of Democratic Transition and Consolidation: Southern Europe, South America, and Post-Communist Europe* (Baltimore, MD: The Johns Hopkins UP, 1996); for a discussion of the Cold War era giving way to a new period of warfare, see Mary Kaldor, *Global Civil Society: An Answer to War* (Cambridge, MA: Polity, 2003); on the 1999 case in which the German government arranged to limit reparations to survivors of slave labor from corporations that collaborated with the Nazi regime, see *Burger-Fischer v. Degussa*, 65 F. Supp. 2d 248; Eduardo Mendieta, "The Ethics of Globalization and the Globalization of Ethics," *Latin American Perspectives on Globalization: Ethics, Politics, and Alternative Visions*, edited by Mario Saenz

(Lanham, MD: Rowman & Littlefield, 2002); Jonathan Glover, *Humanity: A Moral History of the Twentieth Century* (New Haven, CT and London: Yale UP, 2000); Robert O. Keohane, "Global Governance and Accountability," *Taming Globalization: Frontiers of Governance*, edited by David Held and Mathias Koenig-Archibugi (Cambridge, MA: Polity, 2003); on the point that the moral intuitions on which we normally rely upon to guide our actions toward the world's poor are in disarray, see Samuel Scheffler, *Boundaries and Allegiances: Problems of Justice and Responsibility in Liberal Thought* (New York: Oxford UP, 2001); on the point that state corruption is the source of crimes against humanity, see Richard Vernon, "What Is Crime against Humanity?" *Journal of Political Philosophy*, vol. 10, no. 3 (September 2002); Onora O'Neill, *Bounds of Justice* (New York: Cambridge UP, 2000); Philip Gourevitch, *We Wish to Inform You That Tomorrow We Will Be Killed with Our Families: Stories from Rwanda* (New York: Farrar, Straus, and Giroux, 1998); on the unintended link between human rights advocacy and militarism, see David Chandler, "The Road to Military Humanitarianism: How the Human Rights NGOs Shaped a New Humanitarian Agenda," *Human Rights Quarterly*, vol. 23, no. 3 (August 2001); David A. Crocker, "Punishment, Reconciliation, and Democratic Deliberation," *Buffalo Criminal Law Review*, vol. 5 (2002); the observation by Hannah Arendt occurs in Eric B. Gorham, *The Theater of Politics: Hannah Arendt, Political Science, and Higher Education* (Lanham, MD: Lexington Books, 2000); Mandy Jacobson, *Calling the Ghosts* (Executive Producer: Julia Ormond; Directed by Mandy Jacobson and Karmen Jelincic, 1996, 63 min.) and *The Arusha Tapes* (video, 2001); William Kentridge, *History of the Main Complaint* (1994, four-minute animated film) and *Ubu and the Truth Commission* (published by Jane Taylor, Cape Town, South Africa: University of Cape Town Press, 1998); J. M. Coetzee, "History of the Main Complaint," *William Kentridge* (New York: Phaidon, 1999); on distinctions between contemporary cultural reenactments and ancient public theater, see Rush Rehm, *Radical Theatre: Greek Tragedy and the Modern World* (London: Duckworth, 2003); for a discussion of the role of cultural reenactments of war crimes and truth commissions in broadening the meaning of complicity and responsibility, see Stephen L. Esquith, "Re-enacting Mass Violence," *Polity*, vol. 35, no. 4 (July 2003); the point that audiences should acknowledge the suffering others but not fall into the trap of bringing attention to their own capacity for sympathy, see Elizabeth V. Spelman, *Fruits of Sorrow: Framing Our Attention to Suffering* (Boston: Beacon Press, 1997).

Tolerating the Intolerable: The Case of Female Genital Mutilation

Xiaorong Li

Recently, when a hospital in Seattle revealed its plans to design a medically safe clitoridectomy, the public reacted with such outrage that the plans were abandoned. In the Boston area, doctors at the African Women's Health Practice (part of the obstetrics and gynecology department at Brigham and Women's Hospital) champion efforts to ban the practice globally but at the same time treat Somali immigrants suffering complications from the procedure.

A little known legislative act, passed in 1996, makes performing clitoridectomy on underage persons in the US illegal, implying that adults are free to undergo the procedure. At the same time, however, US policy condemns the practice in other countries. The US has granted asylum to some who have fled their home countries in fear that the surgery would be forced upon them. In a celebrated decision, the US Immigration Appeal Court in 1996 granted political asylum to Fauziya Kassinga, a nineteen-year-old citizen of Togo, who had been sheltered from forced clitoridectomy by her father, a wealthy businessman, until his death.

In advocating a policy that condemns the practice abroad, the US seems at least in part to rely on the view held by international human rights organizations and the United Nations. They call for an end to female circumcision worldwide, insisting that it is a violation of women's human rights. (Some assert that "female circumcision" is a

33

euphemism and insist that the practice more precisely be described as "female genital mutilation." This chapter hereafter refers to the practice as FC/FGM.) International human rights advocates and some liberal philosophers insist that one standard must be applied in all places: because FC/FGM violates human rights, it must be banned both abroad and in the US.

But not everyone agrees with this single-standard approach, and some support a different single standard. Cultural relativists, for instance, insist that one should tolerate both abroad and at home *any* practice that is meaningful to a culture—and thus FC/FGM should be accepted worldwide. Complicating matters further, American public sentiment at times seems to reject both views, and instead expresses support for a dual standard: the public seems to want to prohibit FC/FGM in liberal societies, but it is reluctant to intervene in other societies where the practice is part of the culture.

Not only does the apparent inconsistency in the domestic and international positions of the US require explanation, but its inconsistent position also raises a broader question. One must ask what a liberal constitutional state—such as the US—should do when cultural customs offensive to the liberal conscience and values of (most of) its citizens are practiced either in countries *outside* its jurisdiction or in minority communities *within* it. This question will become an increasingly salient public policy issue since, as the community of emigres expands, those who value controversial traditions will want to practice them in an adopted country.

This chapter rejects the notion that a single standard applies in all cases, and explores yet another possibility, suggested by the 1996 legislation. The chapter makes the case for a dual standard. That is, one can reasonably support international efforts for a global ban on FC/FGM, while at the same time urging toleration of the ritual in liberal democratic societies.

To make this case, the chapter first presents a hypothetical scenario to bring to light an ambiguity in the 1996 legislative act concerning the US position toward FC/FGM. The chapter then outlines the arguments for two very different and incompatible attitudes toward FC/FGM. Human rights advocates argue for a global ban on FC/FGM, while cultural relativists insist that the practice should be tolerated. The chapter next turns to two accounts of liberalism, and here too conclusions differ. Liberal feminism supports a ban on FC/FGM; a second liberal argument, sometimes termed "liberal cosmopolitanism," favors toleration of the practice in other cultures but allows for its ban in liberal societies. Critically examining these philosophical positions allows one to reasonably support the reverse of the liberal cosmopolitan standard—that is, liberal states *should oppose FC/FGM practiced abroad but tolerate it at home.*

Dual Standards at Home and Abroad

The World Health Organization has distinguished four types of FC/FGM, ranging from the most thorough excision of female genitalia to a less drastic ritual cutting. Depending on what type of FC/FGM is performed, the immediate health consequences of the procedure can include such complications as pain and bleeding that can lead to hemorrhage and even death. Long-term consequences can include irreversible loss of the clitoris, and possibly the outer and inner labia. Chronic infection, infertility, difficult pregnancy and childbirth, as well as painful sexual intercourse and menstruation are also common permanent effects of the procedure.

To better understand the complex ethical issues and often conflicting sentiments that surround FC/FGM, consider the following scenario. Imagine X, an adult female citizen of the United States, who strongly desires to assert her cultural affiliation and believes that by undergoing FC/FGM she signals her fidelity to a notion of female chastity and ideal womanhood shared by her community. (For the sake of argument, it is irrelevant whether X was born into, has inherited, or has converted to the tradition.) Along with other like-minded persons—most likely first or second generation immigrants from countries where FC/FGM is widely practiced—she hopes to establish the tradition in her adopted country.

To bring the salient elements of the case into stark relief, one must allow three further assumptions. First, one must accept that X is of a normal frame of mind, i.e., she is psychologically fit and suffers from no recognizable psychological disorder involving, for instance, impulses for self-mutilation. She also is capable of understanding general health information and making day-to-day decisions. Second, it is important to assume that, in theory if not in practical application, X—like all women in the US—enjoys full constitutional rights and has recourse to legal protection from persecution if she chooses not to undergo FC/FGM or if she wants to leave her cultural group. She also enjoys a full range of socioeconomic opportunities, including the freedom to marry the person of her choice. (We may further assume that adults in the larger society are generally reluctant to choose circumcised women as wives or sexual partners. Thus, X understands that undergoing FC/FGM means that her choice of partners may be limited to those who share her traditional values.) One must assume, finally, that X enjoys access to medical technology and facilities that allow her doctors to perform the procedure safely and with minimal adverse health consequences. Presented in this way, the case of X raises the following question: Should the liberal society tolerate X's choice to undergo FC/FGM and refrain from intervening with those who assist in the surgery?

Although no woman has relied on the US courts to assert her right to undergo the procedure, the 1996 "Federal Prohibition of Female Genital Mutilation Act" denies FC/FGM only to women under eighteen years of age. But the Act raises many questions. It authorizes US representatives at international financial institutions to "use the voice and vote of the United States to oppose any loan or other utilization of the funds of their respective institution, other than to address basic human needs" for any government or country, which "(1) has, as a cultural custom, a known history of the practice of female genital mutilation; and (2) has not taken steps to implement educational programs designed to prevent the practice of female genital mutilation." The Act mandates that the US refuse loans to countries in which FC/FGM is commonplace but offers no assistance for programs aimed at empowering women and girls. The Act is also too blunt, drawing no distinction between surgeries performed on women and those performed on minors.

As important, it is hard to know how to apply the Act to the US domestic scene. Were X to rely on the Act to support her desire to pursue FC/FGM in the US, a firestorm would likely result. The Act is absolute in its condemnation of the practice abroad, but little thought seems to have been given to defending its implicit permission for adults in the US. The remainder of this chapter argues that there exist morally plausible considerations that support the dual standard suggested in the 1996 Act. That is, X should be permitted to choose FC/FGM in liberal constitutional states, while the procedure ought to be prohibited in countries where basic rights are in jeopardy and women are systematically discriminated against and subjugated. To make this case, it is useful first to turn to two philosophical positions that insist on a single standard: international human rights advocates support a worldwide ban on FC/FGM; cultural relativists contend that the practice should be tolerated globally.

The International Human Rights Argument for Global Prohibition of FC/FGM

In advocating a global ban on FC/FGM, the international human rights camp does *not* stress that the practice offends the liberal moral conscience, nor does it insist that FC/FGM is an extension of cultural beliefs about female inferiority and subjugation. Instead, it contends that FC/FGM is an act of violence—often forced upon girls and women—which threatens lives and health. It insists that the practice violates the basic right to be free from degrading, cruel, and inhumane treatment.

The human rights camp has a convincing case, particularly when one realizes that FC/FGM is routinely forced on girls as young as four or five years old, and the practice is sustained through social coercion. Most would conclude that young girls cannot offer their free consent based on a full understanding of the consequences of the procedure. Though older girls might better understand the health consequences of the ritual, their dependence on their family, friends, and a social network—the same group that also demands that they undergo FC/FGM—effectively bars them from offering their free consent.

The issue of informed consent is a complicated one, however. In general, parents should be trusted to make decisions to promote the well-being of their children. Those who choose FC/FGM for a daughter often consider the ritual necessary to secure her social acceptance and socioeconomic security. (It is also common for parents and relatives to restrain girls during the procedure and to hunt for them if they escape.) Adults who elect to undergo FC/FGM prior to their marriage, or after the birth of their first child, may also see the surgery as a means to secure their social status. However, to argue that these instances represent informed or free actions ignores the fact that those who refuse the procedure—for themselves or their female relatives—are guaranteed an equally, or more, painful life of economic deprivation and social ostracism.

One cannot be said to have real choices if the options are so few and so bleak. So long as the basic political and social structures of some societies remain patriarchal—girls and women continue to face unequal access to education, are allowed only restricted employment outside the home (if employment is allowed at all), and must rely on marriage and motherhood for their livelihood—decisions to undergo FC/FGM are not freely made.

However, no one—citizens of liberal states included—enjoys complete freedom of choice. In the US, for instance, the choice to diet or undergo cosmetic surgery is undoubtedly conditioned by dominant social (and often media-driven) notions of beauty, and thus these "choices" also are not made in complete freedom. But there is a morally significant difference between *having no choice* about one's basic security and life prospects without undergoing FC/FGM on the one hand and, on the other, *finding it difficult* to resist or escape from the pressure of socially dominant notions of beauty. Women in the US can live good lives without surrendering to such social pressures, but women in many societies who escape FC/FGM are denied socioeconomic security and fear that their choice will be overturned by force.

Another critique of the conventional approach by human rights groups is that legal bans on FC/FGM have proven ineffective in the absence of measures to address the inequities that perpetuate the practice in the first place. Although the governments of the Sudan and Egypt banned FC/FGM in the 1940s and 1950s, one finds little evidence of decline in the number of procedures performed, or of improvement in the legal and socioeconomic status of women. Today, from 60% to 90% of all women and girls undergo FC/FGM in those African countries where the practice is traditional, *regardless whether the practice is legal or not*. Futher, prosecution of those who take part in FC/FGM only compounds the problem, driving the practice underground to be performed in unsafe conditions.

An effective campaign against FC/FGM on human rights grounds requires the recognition that undesirable consequences of the practice are worsened by the absence of structural protection of women's basic rights. Such practices can be called "structure sensitive," and FC/FGM is but one example of a structure-sensitive practice. Although not all structure-sensitive practices violate the basic rights of women, all *structure-insensitive* practices do. Widow burning, honor killing, wartime rape and marital rape, domestic violence, and female infanticide, for instance, constitute serious and direct violations of women's vital human rights wherever they occur. Their harms are not mitigated by general political, social, economic, or structural conditions. (US courts at times have accepted a "cultural defense" in cases involving, for instance, the murder of wives by jealous husbands, or the arranged marriages of underage daughters. Such defenses are problematic because they tolerate practices that involve the violation of basic rights, despite the fact that the societies in which these harms occur guarantee those basic rights.) This article contends that FC/FGM is a structure-sensitive practice whose effects can be mitigated in a liberal society. To make this case, however, it is important to examine another approach to FC/FGM—that of the cultural relativist.

The Cultural Relativist Argument for Unconditional Tolerance of FC/FGM

Cultural relativists insist that traditional practices must be understood in cultural context, a crucial element ignored by the human rights camp. University of Chicago anthropologist Richard A. Shweder, for instance, along with a team of legal and cultural scholars, has advocated the broadest tolerance of cultural differences in the United States and elsewhere. Shweder and his colleagues propose fundamental changes to American law in order to accommodate numerous practices—including FC/FGM—so long as they can be demonstrated to promote some social or cultural good.

Cultural relativists claim that any attempt to criminalize cultural practices such as FC/FGM in the US is nothing but an "official attempt to force compliance with the cultural norms of American middle class life." Since American liberal moral norms stem from the value systems of many cultures, no single system can claim priority on modernity, progress, and rationality, or insist that it exercises a culturally neutral point of view.

But the cultural relativist urges toleration of many practices—in other societies as well as in minority communities within liberal societies—even though they may seem offensive from a "Western" point of view. The cultural relativist also draws no distinctions between structure-sensitive and structure-insensitive practices. Their position inevitably leads to the view that not only is FC/FGM tolerable but so are, perhaps, widow burning, honor killing, and female infanticide—any practice, in fact, so long as it has cultural or religious roots.

But the relativist call for tolerating other cultures has trouble contending with disputes about a practice that arise *within* a culture. For instance, members of the same communities that are home to FC/FGM commonly condemn the ritual. Since the 1960s, doctors in the Sudan, Somalia, and Nigeria have documented and publicized the harmful consequences of the procedure. Arguing that the practice deviates from their own religious norms, local scholars and activists challenge interpretations of the Koran or hadith (sayings attributed to the prophet Muhammad) that support FC/FGM in Islamic societies. In Egypt, for instance, opponents of FC/FGM ask how parents can obey the command of the Koran to protect their children, who are God's blessings, and yet subject their daughters to the pain and medical risk of FC/FGM. Others wonder why a woman's genitalia must be excised, since her anatomy is God's creation. Opponents also argue that since FC/FGM jeopardizes a woman's health, it cannot be considered a *sunna*, or good religious action. They argue that the ritual violates the command of the Islamic faith to seek the welfare of all its adherents.

Since intra-cultural disputes are common, the "outsider" must decide *whose* values or interests in the divided cultural community should be tolerated. But in choosing to tolerate the majority view, one risks recognizing a locally dominant faction, which likely can enforce controversial practices and subjugate the vulnerable. As important, the cultural relativist who urges toleration of any culturally based practice within a liberal society endangers the very existence of that society. While tolerance is a value that has shaped the liberal constitutional structure of the US, a liberal society is *not* obliged to tolerate practices incompatible with it. If FC/FGM harms basic liberal constitutional institutions, then the state's commitment to tolerance must become a lesser priority. Advocating unbounded toleration compromises the commitment of liberal states to secure the lives and equal liberties of citizens.

How Morally Significant Are Cultural Boundaries?

Both the international human rights perspective and the cultural relativist support applying a single standard in their treatment of cultural practices in liberal and nonliberal societies (although they reach different conclusions about *what* that standard should be). However, both views are too doctrinaire in their understanding of the moral significance of cultural boundaries—human rights advocates tend to argue that claims to cultural relevancy *in no way* inform the morality of a practice; cultural relativists insist that cultural relevancy is the *most important* consideration.

Another view recognizes that cultural differences between liberal and nonliberal societies are morally significant, and consequently liberal moral standards *in some circumstances* must be suspended in judging cultural practices. Two liberal political philosophers, John Rawls and Michael Walzer, have developed versions of "liberal cosmopolitanism," which (simplified here because of space considerations) espouse this view.

Both are reluctant to allow liberal states to intervene in societies with illiberal practices, unless those practices violate basic, or "urgent" human rights. For them "basic" or "urgent" rights include the right to life and basic liberties, and the freedom from slavery, genocide, and mass expulsion. So long as no violation of this kind occurs, Rawls and Walzer counsel the liberal state to tolerate the cultural practices of other societies, even if those practices would—or should—be prohibited according to liberal constitutional standards. According to this approach, while US intervention in sovereign states practicing genocide is permissible, coercive policies intended to extinguish cultural practices are objectionable. Those holding this view thus might oppose withholding loans to countries with no programs for educating women about FC/FGM—precisely what is advocated in the 1996 law.

In urging toleration of practices abroad that one might not tolerate at home, Rawls and Walzer recognize that one's own (liberal) culture might not be able to discern or understand the moral judgments of other cultures. But neither thinker would accept that a culture could offer any kind of moral justification for the violation of human rights. This reveals that their view is actually based on a context-based assessment of harms. Structure-sensitive practices such as FC/FGM can lead to grave violations of basic human rights in countries where these rights are not secure. But the harms of such practices are likely to be minor where these rights are systematically safeguarded. What renders FC/FGM tolerable or intolerable from a cosmopolitan liberal perspective has little to do with some kind of *cultural* justification; rather, the extent of harm resulting from FC/FGM—and whether those harms rise to the level of basic rights violations—depend, to a large extent, on the different basic political structures in these societies.

Liberal Feminist Arguments for Intolerance

It is important at this juncture to examine a second kind of liberal argument, one that is in tension with the Rawls-Walzer liberal cosmopolitan account. Some liberal feminists argue that even the most "enlightened" practice of FC/FGM is entirely inconsistent with the support of women's equal rights and liberties. These feminists insist that any cultural community that practices sex-based discrimination cannot enjoy support from a liberal constitutional state, and such practices cannot be tolerated abroad. FC/FGM is particularly deplorable, in their view, because sexist beliefs underlie the practice. Supporters of FC/FGM commonly point to the necessity of controlling female sexuality and upholding patriarchal society. Further, the procedure is often performed at men's insistence. The liberal feminist contends that, for women to enjoy human rights as equal human beings, one must interfere with illiberal or sexist practices *wherever* they occur—even in liberal societies.

Susan Okin, for instance, argues that nonliberal cultures and subcultures should either become extinct or rid themselves of their sexist practices. For Okin, multiculturalism is laudable in a liberal democracy *only if* its minority subcultures can survive such reforms. However, critics of Okin's view routinely suggest that the list of practices she would see abolished is too far-reaching and undiscriminating. She is also criticized for offering no way to morally rank such practices as wearing head scarves or veils, forced child marriage, FC/FGM, polygamy, wife beating, widow burning, and honor killing. Although all of these practices are sexist, critics are troubled by the suggestion that no line can be drawn between *tolerable* sexist and illiberal practices and *intolerable* ones.

According to this view, furthermore, sexist and illiberal practices are no less morally objectionable simply because women *themselves* choose to take part in them. The choice of X to undergo FC/FGM is as morally objectionable as if others coerced her into undergoing the procedure. In fact, the list of practices impermissible for X is extensive—it is also morally unacceptable for her to take part in such sex trades as pornography or prostitution, for her to choose breast augmentation, or for her to diet in hopes of attaining a (likely patriarchally dictated) standard of beauty.

This view challenges the distinction that the nineteenth century moral philosopher John Stuart Mill famously drew between those illiberal practices that harm others and infringe on their liberties without their informed consent, and those that do not. Liberal feminists such as Okin insist that sexist practices are bad for women—regardless of what any particular woman believes is good or meaningful for *herself*. Their view rests on an understanding that the moral worth of a human life is defined by autonomy, individual freedom, and gender equality, and thus a life shaped by sexist beliefs is unworthy of the respect of a liberal state. According to this view, in choosing FC/FGM, X accepts her dehumanization, and she perpetuates a belief system that justifies the social control over women and limits the exercise of their full potential.

Both feminist liberals and political liberals value equal constitutional protection of basic liberties for all citizens. But once those basic liberties are secure, the political liberal urges toleration of illiberal views and practices, while the feminist parts company and insists that illiberal practices have no place in a liberal state, which should promote the morally worthy life defined by liberal values.

A Reasonable Dual Standard

Applying the positions presented thus far to the case of X, the hypothetical women who resides in a liberal society and seeks to undergo FC/FGM, one finds:

1. The **international human rights advocate** argues that FC/FGM violates women's human rights and therefore the practice should be banned in liberal and nonliberal societies alike.

2. Arguing that traditional practices must be understood in cultural context, the **cultural relativist** argues for toleration of FC/FGM in both liberal and nonliberal societies.

3. The **liberal cosmopolitan** is reluctant to justify international intervention to end illiberal (sex-discriminatory) practices in nonliberal societies, so long as no "urgent" human rights are violated; a ban on illiberal practices in liberal societies is permissible.

4. The **liberal feminist** opposes sex-discriminatory practices such as FC/FGM, arguing that these practices have no place in a liberal society.

Political liberalism allows for yet another approach. This approach is based on the recognition that reasonable persons, who enjoy freedom of conscience and expression, will always disagree about conceptions of human nature and notions of the good. Liberal states should allow citizens to practice what they believe so long as their practices do not undermine the basic liberal constitutional structure of the society. By inference, the liberal state should safeguard children from undergoing FC/FGM, since minors cannot offer their informed consent. The liberal state also has an interest in encouraging in girls a sense of their equality, in order that they exercise their equal rights and fulfill their responsibilities as adult citizens. FC/FGM would undermine their developing sense of equal worth. Similar points have been made in strictly enforcing laws banning child pornography and child prostitution in this country, while at the same time laws banning adult prostitution often lack enforcement, indicating a degree of state tolerance.

Applied to the case of X, this understanding of FC/FGM would allow her to decide whether to undergo the procedure—so long as she has full access to medical information, safe medical facilities, and her full range of basic rights are secure. The liberal state must also protect her from physical coercion to undergo FC/FGM, and it must provide the socioeconomic securities that prevent women from "choosing" FC/FGM out of desperation.

This brand of political liberal would not support elimination of public funding to the minority community within a liberal society that allows—but does not coerce—members to practice FC/FGM. The political liberal would not support a ban on the practice, which would communicate to members of the community that their beliefs are not worthy of respect by the liberal state and the society at large. Yet this form of liberalism could—without contradiction—at the same time advocate banning FC/FGM in countries lacking institutional protection of basic, or "urgent," rights.

The case for treating differently FC/FGM internationally and domestically illustrates the importance of taking a structure-sensitive approach to illiberal cultural practices. One must look at the broader circumstances in which a practice is embedded to accurately discern the harm that results from that practice. Consider the difference between FC/FGM and male circumcision. Although both practices seem to fulfill a similar cultural role—as a rite of passage, and to celebrate entry into a community, for instance—and both demand irreversible physical alterations to the body, the two practices are very different. Male circumcision is usually accompanied by brief pain, only rarely harms health, and carries no irreversible loss of sexual or reproductive function. It also does not subjugate men to women or take from men control of their sexuality. Arguing for toleration of FC/FGM worldwide based on the fact that circumcision of males is also a permissible practice ignores a crucial difference between the two practices. Male circumcision is *not* structure sensitive, and its harms are likely to be minor in societies *with* or *without* the structural protection of basic rights. FC/FGM is structure sentitive, and its harms can be magnified when women lack basic rights.

In liberal societies, the harms of FC/FGM can be mitigated. One could argue that adult FC/FGM is comparable to another accepted practice—cosmetic surgery. In this case, individuals (ideally) make informed choices, and the procedure is likely to result in some harm. Yet, one's decision to undergo cosmetic surgery (or FC/FGM) harms no one else, and it does not compromise the liberal state's interest in safeguarding equal basic liberties. However, X's decision is not ethically equivalent to choosing to wear a headscarf, entering into a polygamous marriage, or choosing celibacy (by becoming a nun, for example)—in these cases a woman's decision is reversible and her social compromises need not be permanent. But X's choice to undergo FC/FGM, which involves permanent physical and social changes—just as cosmetic surgery does—should be permitted in a liberal society.

This chapter has made the case that liberal societies should tolerate those illiberal practices that do not violate basic rights, and thus the 1996 Act's dual standard is defensible. It is important to note that X—or any women residing in a liberal society—might consider that FC/FGM is unnecessary for the cultural purposes that it was meant to serve. Certainly, if the meaning of the ritual is to acknowledge the importance of chastity and devotion to husband and children, then other symbolic ceremonies could sufficiently express a woman's commitment to these values. Cultural communities could abandon the traditional practice of FC/FGM and develop other rituals to celebrate rites of passage and to make good-faith pledges. The sincerity of these pledges need not require the disabling of women (or men). And maiming a woman offers no guarantee of her chastity—especially if *she* no longer believes in its value.

The encouraging news is that, as options and opportunities open to women, the socioeconomic incentives for undergoing FC/FGM will disappear. Resistance by women in patriarchal communities also promises to continue. Liberal states can best help women in patriarchal societies and minority communities by supporting institution building and capability-development programs that seek to secure the rights of women and to empower girls. Such measures support domestic initiatives for change within cultural and subcultural communities. Although liberal states should support efforts to ban practices such as FC/FGM in societies that do not protect basic rights, liberal states can afford to tolerate such practices when basic rights are secure. So long as citizens make informed decisions about practices in a way that does not undermine the protection of basic liberties and rights, liberal states should treat these undertakings as expressions of belief and faith.

This chapter appeared previously in *Philosophy & Public Policy Quarterly*, vol. 21, no. 1 (Winter 2001).

Sources

Ben Barker-Benfiled, "Sexual Surgery in Late Nineteenth Century America," *International Journal of Health Services*, vol. 279 (1975); Barbara Crossette, "Testing the Limits of Tolerance as Cultures Mix," *New York Times* (March 6, 1999); Claudia Dreifus, "A Conversation with Nawal Nour: A Life Devoted to Stopping the Suffering of Mutilation," *New York Times* (July 11, 2000); Isabelle R. Gunning, "Arrogant Perception, World-Travelling and Multicultural Feminism: The Case of Female Genital Surgeries," *Columbia Human Rights Law Review*, vol. 23 (1992); the view of Rawls relevant to this discussion can be found in *The Law of Peoples* (Harvard University Press, 1999), and those of Walzer in *Just and Unjust Wars* (Basic Books, 1977); Susan M. Okin, *Is Multiculturalism Bad for Women?* (Princeton University Press, 1999); Martha Nussbaum, "A Plea for Difficulty," in *Female Genital Mutilation: A Guide to Laws and Policies Worldwide*, edited by Anika Rahman and Nahid Toubia (Zed Books, 2000); John Rawls, *Political Liberalism* (Columbia University Press, 1993); Yael Tamir, "Hands Off Clitoridectomy: What Our Revulsion Reveals about Ourselves," *Boston Review*, vol. 21 (1996); Alice Walker and Pratibha Parmar, *Warrior Marks: Female Genital Mutilation and the Sexual Blinding of Women* (Harcourt Brace & Company, 1993); Nadia Wassef and Melron Micol-Wilson, "Ending Female Genital Mutilation without Human Rights: Two Approaches," *Human Rights Dialogue* (Carnegie Council on Ethics and International Affairs, 2000); Michael Walzer, "The Rights of Political Communities," in *Just and Unjust Wars, International Ethics*, edited by Charles Beitz et al. (Princeton University Press, 1985); and *Public Law* 104-208, September 30, 1996 (10th US Congress).

Fighting Child Labor Abroad: Conceptual Problems and Practical Solutions

Roland Pierik

Child labor is a topic that evokes deep emotions and a growing international concern. Most recent ILO estimates show that some 211 million children between 5 and 14 are engaged in some form of economic activity, and 119 million of them are engaged in hazardous work. The poverty implications of child labor are often transmitted from parents to children, a process that is called the *dynastic poverty trap*. If a child has to labor and is therefore insufficiently educated, then as an adult he can only be employed as a low-skilled, low-paid laborer. If his income is insufficient to provide for a family, his children are also forced to work. The vicious cycle thereby continues.

In all Western liberal democracies, child labor is morally condemned, legally forbidden, and virtually nonexistent. This has not always been the case. During the Industrial Revolution, child labor was as widespread in Europe and the United States as it is nowadays in India and Bangladesh. Current debates on child labor within Western societies are closely linked to the increasing importance of globalization and its effects on national governments. One element of globalization is the increasing permeability of national legal and political orders. The import of commodities produced by child labor into Western states refers to practices outside their territory, which nevertheless conflict with its prevailing norms and values.

One finds a near consensus in Western liberal democracies that child labor is a deplorable practice that should be abandoned. Rejecting child labor on moral terms is one thing; fighting it, however, is quite another matter. What, if anything, should governments of affluent societies do to combat child labor?

The problem is that the directness of our intuitions does not automatically translate into straightforward certainty about ways to fight the problem. One complication is that the Western opposition against child labor is usually based on an implicit conception of childhood that is not always embraced in countries in which most child labor occurs. A second complication is that not all work for children is inherently bad. This chapter distinguishes *child work*, activities that take the child's growth and development into account, from *child labor,* which is harmful because it hinders children's physical, psychological, emotional, or social development. Finally, not every Western action against child labor is ipso facto in the best interest of the children involved. This has been shown by an example that has gained notoriety. In 1995 the US Congress considered the Child Labor Deterrence Bill (which came to be known as Harkin's bill after Senator Tom Harkin, democratic senator from Iowa, one of its sponsors) that sought to forbid the import of products made with the involvement of workers under the age of 15. Supporters of this bill hoped (and expected) that such a boycott would result in these children returning to school. Soon after the introduction of the bill, the TV channel NBC broadcasted a documentary showing that Wal-Mart, America's largest retailer, was selling clothing made by child labor in Bangladesh. The visibility of small children producing clothing for the US market shocked both the public and politicians and brought Harkin's bill to the center of attention, not only in the USA. Although the bill was never passed, it caused shockwaves in some countries that mainly export to the United States. For example, the Bangladeshi Garment Manufacturers and Export Association (BGMEA) perceived the discussions in the US Congress as a threat to the export of its products. Nervous factory owners, unwilling to risk access to their most important market, quickly fired around 50,000 children—75% of the total then employed. The expectations in the United States that these children would return to school was not only overly optimistic, it also turned out to be dramatically naive. Development expert Ben White concluded that not one of the dismissed children had gone back to school. Half of them had found other occupations (mainly in informal-sector and street activities, including domestic service, brick-chipping, selling flowers on the street and prostitution) but with greatly reduced earnings while the other half were actively seeking work. The children still working in the garment factories had better nutrition and better health care than those who had been dismissed.

One lesson to be learned here is that economic boycotts are not the best strategy against child labor and, as the example shows, may have even the opposite effects from those intended. Boycotts only affect businesses that export goods, and these only employ 5% of working children. Therefore, trade sanctions against products produced by child labor are unlikely to have a significant effect on the occurrence of child labor. More generally, the lesson is that Western policies toward child labor applied to developing countries should not be based on impulse, emotion, or good intentions but instead on careful analysis and research. Since such policies aim to combat practices in another country, policy makers should be aware of the many pitfalls risked by intervention in the complex interactions of family choices and market structures. Moreover, such policies need to recognize the forces that give rise to child labor in the first place and that will most likely respond to any attempt to intervene.

Two Differences

There exist two differences between Western countries and developing countries that must be taken into account if Western governments are to successfully enact policies against child labor abroad. One cannot emphasize too strongly the importance of socioeconomic differences and cultural differences among developed and developing nations. For one thing, it should be acknowledged that the socioeconomic, political, and infrastructural situation in Bangladesh or India is very different from that in the US or European countries. Policies such as boycotts focus only on the effects of child labor—its products—but typically fail to investigate the structural reasons for the occurrence of child labor, namely poverty.

Prohibition of child labor is a prudent policy only in the presence of alternative ways to provide for, or increase, the family income. Even poor parents do not send their children to work if they can prevent it. Indeed, development scholar Kaushik Basu argues that in very poor regions the alternative to child labor may be very harsh—acute hunger or even starvation. Boycotts as proposed in Harkin's bill are counterproductive: children that work in the "export industry" usually work in comparatively good conditions. If they lose their jobs, and if the reasons why they work are not addressed, they may be forced into worse, more dangerous, and less well paid jobs. Moreover, an important assumption justifying Harkin's bill was that if children do not work, they would automatically return to school. Again, things are more complicated, because parental choices are affected by many factors. Schooling is only a viable alternative for child labor if it is within reach. For one thing, schooling should be affordable and several costs have to be taken into account: direct costs (e.g., school fees) and additional costs (e.g., school uniforms, books, and other materials). A second factor is the quality of education: if it is of poor quality—due to overcrowded or under-funded schools, under-skilled or apathetic teachers, or inadequate sanitation—then it is not a compelling alternative for child labor. A third factor is the accessibility: the physical distance to school should not be too big.

In short, Western policies toward child labor abroad must take account of the many differences between Western and developing countries, and not concoct simple analogies with the effects such policies would have in Western societies. Such policies should be based on good knowledge of the socioeconomic, infrastructural, and political characteristics of the society involved.

A second relevant consideration in these debates concerns the differences between developed and developing nations in prevailing ideas about childhood and the role of work and education therein. The conception of childhood is a subject of fierce and continuing discussions. On one hand, one finds general agreement that childhood can be described as a biologically driven natural phenomenon characterized by physical and mental growth stages. On the other hand, childhood is a social construct, and it is interpreted very differently in various cultural contexts. The Western conceptualization can be characterized in terms of a strict separation of childhood from adulthood. Childhood is seen as a "mythic walled garden" of play and study, marked by special dress and literature. It is inspired by the "myth of childhood innocence" where children are happy and separated form the wicked adult world. It is assumed that growing up requires an extended period of socialization and formalized education in schools. Children are therefore discouraged from participation in adult concerns such as economic maintenance.

However, this Western conceptualization of childhood is atypical. Child work in any form has always been part of a wider set of childhood activities; in fact, child work is the norm in most of the world. It is barred in Western society only as a consequence of harsh work conditions and maltreatment resulting from the Industrial Revolution. The Western conceptualization has changed dramatically since then and is therefore unique in historical context, as much as it is unique in comparison with other non-Western societies.

Much work in non-industrialized sectors in developing countries is organized in workshops or family-owned businesses, not in large-scale, impersonal factories. The fact that these children work alongside their parents protects them against the forms of exploitation that were common during the heyday of the Industrial Revolution. Such family workshops are typically small and non-industrial. Children learn by doing and there is usually no need for formal education beyond the basic level or high school diploma to work in, and succeed one's parents, in the family-owned businesses. Children's acting in the role of adults is seen as an important element in education in such contexts. Moreover, it is taken as an expression of family unity and solidarity—as it was in Western societies prior to the Industrial Revolution. Work is seen as an important means of teaching and socializing children in their middle childhood—approximately between the ages of 6 and 12. In other cases, parents regard on the job training in apprenticeships as a useful activity that both provides an income and trains the child in skills useful for future employment.

Under specific conditions work can be beneficial for children in some societies. Therefore, we must distinguish *child work*—that is an essential and meaningful part of education and socialization—from *child labor*—that is harmful because it prevents children from receiving an education, or hinders their physical, psychological, social, or emotional development. Of course, it is easier to conceptually distinguish both than to give policy recommendations on where to draw the line. However, any successful policy against child labor should bite this bullet. After all, the alternative strategy of not recognizing the distinction between child work and child labor undermines the plausibility of the struggle against child labor—why would one try to abolish necessary sources of socialization and education? Moreover, given the scarcity of energy and means, it is better to set priorities and start fighting the worst forms of child labor.

Let me return to the Western policies against child labor abroad. I have emphasized some important considerations: the difference in socioeconomic and infrastructural situations, different conceptions about childhood, and the distinction between child work and child labor. Harkin's bill had such unfortunate effects because it was based on over-idealistic and impractical assumptions. However, there are also examples of more successful policies on child labor abroad.

Successful Policies against Child Labor

A policy against child labor that recently gained much critical acclaim is rewarding parents financially for sending their children to school. A good example of such a program is *Oportunidades* in Mexico. This program started in 1997 (until March 2002 the program was called PROGRESA) and pays parents if their children go to school, a stipend that increases with the child's age. The education grants are substantial, about two-thirds of what secondary students would receive for full-time work. In addition, families are also given a grant to provide for the additional costs of education. Moreover, these measures are embedded in a more general program, also focusing on health and nutrition. Such conditional cash transfer programs counteract child labor because they both mitigate the family's need for the child's economic contribution and lower the relative return to work. As such the program reduces child labor, increases educational attainment and improves health and nutrition for children and parents. In their evaluation of the program, Skoufias and Parker argue that

> the integrated nature of the program reflects a belief that addressing all dimensions of human capital simultaneously has greater social returns than considering each in isolation. Improved health and nutritional status are not only desirable in themselves, but have an indirect impact through enhancing the effectiveness of education programs, since school attendance and performance are often adversely affected by poor health and nutrition.

The program is effective because it addresses poverty, the root cause of both child labor and low school attendance. In the short term, the program raises family income, lowers the dependence on children's work for the family income, and reduces the cost of attending school. In the long term it can stop the vicious spiral of the dynastic poverty trap, which I discussed in the introduction of this chapter.

Removing the financial limitations of parents enables them to let their children finish their education. If the children enter the labor market as educated laborers they will be able to earn a full family income as adults, making additional income of their own children unnecessary. This enables the next generation also to attend school full time.

Another positive characteristic of the program is that it is administered in a cost-effective manner, with administrative costs of less that 10% of the total budget, which is regarded as quite small, given the complexity of the program. *Oportunidades* seems to be a promising example of a policy against child labor. It not only reduces child labor but also enhances school attention; it is transparent, efficient, and effective.

Even though such programs are cost effective, they might only be partly feasible for governments of developing countries, with little money available. Western governments hoping to curb child labor should support such collaborative measures financially, preferably in cooperation with NGOs who have knowledge of the local situation. A good example of such cooperation can be found in Bangladesh. In the wake of the discussion on Harkin's bill and the sudden dismissal of thousands of children from the garment industry, the Bangladeshi government and garment industry came under intense public scrutiny. This public pressure enabled local NGOs, in cooperation with UNICEF and the ILO, to negotiate a Memorandum of Understanding with the employers (allied in the BGMEA) to phase out child labor. After long and delicate negotiations, a program, more or less similarly to *Oportunidades* in Mexico, has been set up. The work is divided up along competences: the ILO organizes the monitoring system and stipendiums, education facilities are made available by UNICEF, while funding is provided by the US Department of Labor and other Western organizations. Since these programs are targeted to the working children and are efficient, effective, and transparent, cooperation in such programs seems to be a promising option for Western governments that seek to curb child labor abroad.

Five Recommendations

Let me conclude by suggesting five recommendations for Western policy makers that might enable them to avoid pitfalls such as those found in Harkin's bill.

Act collectively. Child labor is a global problem, and can only be fought on a global scale. Policies against child labor can only be successful if they are the result of international cooperation. Even large countries such as the United States cannot achieve much on their own. Policies must encourage multinational corporations to formulate codes of conduct towards child labor. Governments should also work together in international and supranational organizations such as UNICEF and the ILO. They should cooperate with (international) NGOs that have experience in the field, and support promising projects, as happened in Bangladesh.

Act contextually. There is no single simple policy measure that can end child labor. Policies that have been very successful in one context did not work in another context, or even had contrary effects. Before proposing a specific policy, policy makers should be aware of the socioeconomic and infrastructural characteristics of the society involved. Since there exists an emerging body of empirical literature on the effects of different policies against child labor in developing countries, policies should be based on the available information, instead of intuition or good faith.

Policies should be based on an inclusive conception of childhood. Although the Western idea of childhood is very atypical, it has been used as a universal model in many conventions, such as those of the ILO. As such, this biased conception has dominated most international discussions on child labor and children's rights. The fight against child labor would be strengthened if conventions and policies were based on a more inclusive conception of childhood, including non-Western ideas on the balance between work and education in socialization. Moreover, one can question whether the romanticized ideal of childhood underlying international conventions is still valid even for Western societies. Indeed, it is an extreme position to argue that delivering newspapers, babysitting, or mowing the lawn after school is an intolerable infringement on someone's childhood. The abolitionist argument, that child employment is ipso facto an offence against childhood, is based on a romantic conception of childhood that is even outdated in Western societies today.

More sensitivity to culture and the way it mediates the effects of experience on children is not the same as defending cultural relativism, or discouraging international action against child labor. Instead, defending a more inclusive conception of childhood as the basis of policies against child labor takes into account a broader representation of human experience than those found in Euro-American values that are currently used.

Do not propose a global ban on all child labor. Some abolition-ist groups argue that all child labor should be banned globally, and that we have only succeeded if all children in the world receive full-time formal education. However, such policy goals are entirely unre-alistic, strategically counterproductive and, as a result, more harmful than they are helpful. There are more than 200 million child laborers today, and the practice has persisted for more than two centuries. This is a huge and complex problem that cannot be solved overnight. Of course, child labor is not desirable in an ideal world. However, aboli-tionist goals are entirely unrealistic and strategically counterproduc-tive in our non-ideal world. As a result, they do more harm than good. Instead of an abolitionist approach, Western governments should embrace a gradualist approach, ranking several forms of child labor on the basis of harmfulness, making a priority the banning of the worst forms, and proposing different policies for different forms of child labor.

We must first distinguish child work—that is part of education and socialization—from child labor—that is harmful for children. Next, the category of child labor should be divided in the uncondi-tionally worst form of child labor and other forms of child labor. The unconditionally worst form of child labor includes work that hinders the physical, psychological, and social development of children. Work in unhealthy and dangerous environments, full-time work for young children, and working too many hours a day also are among the worst forms of child labor. Most attention should be given to an outright ban of these worst forms of child labor. Although such a ban might have negative effects on the poorest families in the short run, it seems pointless to allow dangerous labor for children who cannot properly assess the long-term damage these jobs can cause (and whose parents also may be unable to make such an assessment). Governments should take collective action to single out these worst forms and cre-ate, implement, and monitor internationally accepted norms to abol-ish them. A good example is ILO Convention 182 (1999) that defines and prohibits the worst forms of child labor. The change of terminol-ogy is evident: from a rhetoric notion like the "total abolition of child labor" in the earlier conventions to a limitation of, and focus on, the worst forms thereof.

Distinguishing the unconditionally worst form of child labor from less harmful forms implies that the latter, at least for the near future, may have to be tolerated. Toleration does not imply indifference but a sense of realism. If we cannot ban all child labor we should prioritize on the worst forms. Moreover, banning is not the only policy available. Not rigidly fixing on a ban enables policy makers to consider alternatives, for example, policies to improve the working conditions, or policies that combine part-time work for these children with part-time education.

Do not only focus on legal coercive measures, but also consider collaborative measures. Most policies against child labor take the form of coercive measures intended to forbid child labor legally. Harkin's bill, for example, proposed a legal prohibition of the importation of commodities made by child labor. Coercive measures are important but have to be used carefully; they should be applied only against the worst forms of child labor. Besides legal measures, Western governments could also engage in collaborative initiatives. Such initiatives should be designed to alter the (economic) environment of decision makers (parents and employers), rendering them more willing to let children stay out of work and spend more time on schooling and other activities. These measures do not necessarily need a legislative backup. Collaborative measures are more appropriate for those forms of child labor that are less urgent. Since parents typically want to keep their children out of the workplace and in school, collaborative measures are more successful than legal bans on child labor. The *Oportunidades* program discussed above provides a good example of such a collaborative policy. However, such policies might not be feasible for governments of developing countries, with little money for such incentives. Western governments hoping to curb child labor would do well to support collaborative measures financially by, for instance, fighting poverty, raising the income of parents so that the children don't have to work, supporting policies that keep children in schools, building schools, and many other initiatives.

Child labor today is not an isolated phenomenon in developing countries because, as a result of globalization, all states in the contemporary world are connected in one global economy. Child labor is a symptom of current global inequality, and Western states are not innocent bystanders. The fight against child labor should not be separated from the issue of global inequality. Any action by Western governments against child labor is futile, implausible, and not reciprocal if that action does not also reflect their own responsibility in creating and sustaining child labor. Western governments should accept that child labor is a complex issue and set as a priority elimination of its worst forms. At the same time, however, Western governments must focus not only on legal coercive measurements but also embrace collaborative measurements. Indeed, increasing development assistance, for example, for programs like *Oportunidades*, is among the best policy options to successfully end child labor.

Author's Note: This chapter is an elaboration of my "Child Labor Abroad: Five Policy Options," *Philosophy & Public Policy Quarterly*, vol. 24, no. 3 (Summer 2004). I thank Verna V. Gehring and Ingrid Robeyns for their constructive comments on various versions of this paper and Mijke Houwerzijl for collaboration on a related project.

Sources

On child labor in general, see Kaushik Basu, "Child Labor: Cause, Consequence, and Cure, with Remarks on International Labor Standards," *Journal of Economic Literature* 37 (1999); Kausik Basu and Zafris Tzannatos, "The Global Child Labor Problem: What Do We Know and What Can We Do?" *The World Bank Economic Review*, vol. 17, no. 2 (2003); Runa Begum, *Elimination of Child Labour from the Export Garment Industry of Bangladesh: An Experience of Western Intervention* (University of Birmingham, 2003); A. James and A. Prout (editors), *Constructing and Reconstructing Childhood: Contemporary Issues in the Sociological Study of Childhood* (Falmer Press, 1997); Alec Fyfe, *Child Labor* (Polity Press, 1997); Christiaan Grootaert, *The Policy Analysis of Child Labor: A Comparative Study* (Macmillan Press, 1999); Jane Humphries, "Child Labor: Lessons from the Historical Experience of Today's Industrial Economies," *The World Bank Economic Review* 17 (2003); Jane Humphries, "Child Labor: Lessons from the Historical Experience of Today's Industrial Economies," *The World Bank Economic Review* 17 (2003); William E. Myers, "The Right Rights? Child Labor in a Globalizing World," *Annals* 575 (May 2001); Debra Satz, "Child Labor: A Normative Perspective," *The World Bank Economic Review* 17 (2003); Ben White, "Globalization and the Child Labor Problem," *Journal of International Development*, vol. 8, no. 6 (1996); UNICEF, *The State of the World's Children 1997* (Oxford University Press, 1997). For information on the Progresa program, see Alan B. Krueger, "Putting Development Dollars to Use, South of the Border," *New York Times* (May 2, 2002); Emmanuel Skoufias and Susan W. Parker, "Conditional Cash Transfers and Their Impact on Child Work and Schooling," *Economia*, vol. 2, no. 1 (2001). For evaluations of the program (carried out by The International Food Policy Research Institute in Washington) see www.ifpri.org/themes/progresa.htm.

Development Ethics and Globalization

David A. Crocker

Development—conceived generally as desired or desirable social change—is the work of policymakers, project managers, grassroots communities, and international aid donors, all of whom confront daily moral questions in their work with poor countries. Seeking explicit and reasoned answers to those questions is the particular work of development philosophers and other ethicists. Among the general questions they address are the following: What should be meant by "development"? In what direction and by what means should a society "develop"? Who is morally responsible for beneficial change? What are the obligations, if any, of rich societies to poor societies? How should globalization's impact and potential be assessed ethically? The purpose of this chapter is to outline briefly the history of development ethics and then discuss what the moral assessments of development reveal about globalization and its challenges.

A Brief History of Development Ethics

Development ethics traces its beginnings to the last half of the twentieth century. In the 1940s, activists and social critics—such as Mohandas Gandhi in India, Raul Prebisch in Latin America, and Frantz Fanon in Africa—criticized colonialism and orthodox economic development. In the early 1960s, American Denis Goulet—influenced by French economist Louis-Joseph Lebret and social scientists such as Gunner Myrdal—championed the view that development must be "redefined, de mystified, and thrust into the arena of moral debate." Goulet also insisted that because what is called "development" so often increases human suffering, development can amount to "anti-development."

In the 1970s, Peter Singer's utilitarian arguments for famine relief and Garrett Hardin's "lifeboat ethics" fueled debates about whether affluent nations (or their citizens) have moral obligations to aid starving people in poor countries and—if they do—to establish the basis and extent of those obligations. By the early eighties, consensus formed in arguing that financial relief and food aid only partly addressed the problems of hunger, poverty, underdevelopment, and international injustice. Development ethicists began insisting on a more comprehensive, empirically informed, and policy-relevant "ethics of Third World development." These ethicists also began to recognize that ethical assessment must include sensitivity to a society's culture, including its values.

Contemporary development ethicists—Paul Streeten and Amartya Sen are two notable examples—address such problems as global economic inequality, hunger, and underdevelopment by explicitly applying ethical principles. Building on Streeten's work, Sen argues that development cannot be understood as economic growth, industrialization, or modernization, which are at best means, but must be viewed fundamentally as the expansion of people's "valuable capabilities and functionings:

> The valued functionings can vary from such elementary ones as avoiding mortality or preventable morbidity, or being sheltered, clothed, and nourished, to such complex achievements as taking part in the life of the community, having a joyful and stimulating life, or attaining self-respect and the respect of others.

Consensus and Disagreement

Development ethicists typically make explicit and seek systematic answers to a number of related questions: What should count as (good) development? Should one continue to speak of "development" instead of, for example, "progress," "transformation," "liberation," or "post-development alternatives to development"? What basic economic, political, and cultural goals and strategies should a region, nation, or community pursue, and what principles should inform their selection? What moral issues emerge in development policymaking and practice, and how should they be resolved? Who (or what institutions) bear responsibility for preventing or bringing about development—a nation's government, civil society, or the market? What role—if any—should more affluent states, international institutions, and nongovernmental associations and individuals have in the self-development of poor countries? What is the role of citizens? What are the most serious local, national, and international impediments to good development? How is "globalization" to be understood, and what moral assessments can be given of its promises and risks? Who should decide these questions and by what methods? What are the roles of theoretical reflection and public deliberation?

Development ethicists aim not merely to understand the nature, causes, and consequences of development, but they also promote specific conceptions. Aware that what has been called "development" has created as many problems as it has solved, development ethicists generally agree that development projects and aid givers must aim to achieve both human well-being and a healthy environment. Economic growth, industrialization, and modernization that result in a high or improving gross domestic product may not necessarily promote "good" development. Most development ethicists would reject two models of "development": (1) economic growth as the increase of opulence without regard to an increase in human living conditions (what Sen and Jean Drèze call "unaimed opulence") and (2) development in which physical needs are satisfied at the expense of political liberties.

Development ethicists also believe that an accurate assessment of development requires the scrutiny of ethicists of many nationalities and cultural identities in order to be culturally sensitive to the needs and concerns of different societies, and to properly determine whether efforts toward development alleviate deprivation worldwide.

Despite their many points of agreement, development ethicists also continue to consider a number of unsettled issues, one of which is the scope of development ethics. Although development ethics originated as the "ethics of Third World Development," and development ethicists tend to agree that the "First-Second-Third World" trichotomy should be eliminated, there exists no consensus about whether development ethics should extend beyond its central concern of assessing the development needs of poor societies. Some agree that human deprivation exists in rich countries and regions, and therefore these "underdeveloped" areas properly fall within the scope of development ethics. Others suggest that the socioeconomic model that the developed northern hemisphere has been exporting to the less developed South results in the underdevelopment of both. Still others insist that attention to pockets of deprivation within developed nations of the North or West only serves to divert attention from the world's most destitute countries and regions.

Among other unresolved debates, development ethicists argue over whether rich countries should restrict themselves to direct assistance to a poor country, or whether more diffuse involvement—in migration and environmental treaties, for instance—is also justifiable. Also unresolved remains whether development ethics should address such topics as trade, the Internet, drug trafficking, military intervention, the conduct of war, peace keeping, and the proposed international criminal court when—or to the extent that—these topics have no causal relationship to absolute or relative poverty.

A final, but important, unresolved issue that divides development ethicists is the status of various moral norms. Among the numerous positions that have emerged, two are dominant. One group, "universalists" (who embrace such ethical approaches as utilitarianism and deontology), argue that development goals and principles are valid for all societies. But another group, "particularists" (who tend to favor communitarianism and postmodern relativism), commonly reply that universalism masks ethnocentrism and (Northern or Western) cultural imperialism. Particularists either reject the existence of universal principles or affirm only the *procedural* principle that each nation or society should draw on its own traditions and decide its own development ethic and path. Some approaches (including one advanced, for instance, by Amartya Sen, Martha Nussbaum, Jonathan Glover, Seyla Benhabib, and this author) try to avoid the standoff between universalists and particularists by insisting that development ethics can forge a cross-cultural consensus in which a political community's own freedom to make development choices is one among a plurality of fundamental norms.

Important areas of further work include addressing the question of *which* moral notion ought to have priority in understanding and securing human well-being and development. Among many candidates, some advocate utility or preference satisfaction as most fundamental, others suggest that income and wealth are most important, and still others advocate autonomy. Capability ethicists, such as Sen and Nussbaum, emphasize valuable and valued human freedoms (capabilities) and achievements ("functionings").

Development Ethics and Globalization

A new and pressing task faced by development ethics is the ethical evaluation of "globalization." As with the term "development" in the 1960s, in the 1990s, "globalization" has become a cliché and buzzword celebrated by the mainstream and condemned by dissenters. Among the crucial questions development ethicists must answer are as follows: What is globalization, and what are the salient interpretations of its possible effects? Is it likely to result in the demise, resurgence, or transformation of state power? Will it eliminate, accentuate, or transform the power inequities between the developed Northern hemisphere and the less developed Southern hemisphere? Does globalization (or some of its different varieties) undermine, constrain, enable, or promote ethically defensible development? Can and should globalization be resisted, contested, modified, or transformed?

One informal, but helpful, definition of globalization has been offered by David Held, Anthony McGrew, David Goldblatt, and Jonathan Perraton:

> Globalization may be thought of as the widening, deepening and speeding up of worldwide interconnectedness in all aspects of contemporary social life, from the cultural to the criminal, the financial to the spiritual.

Although the effects of globalization's interconnectedness are vigorously debated, three main interpretations have emerged, which may be labeled (1) hyperglobalism, (2) skepticism, and (3) transformationalism.

Hyperglobalism. Economist Jadish Bhagwati and journalist Thomas L. Friedman exemplify the hyperglobalist position, which conceives of globalization as a worldwide age of economic (capitalist) integration characterized by open trade, global financial flows, and the triumph of multinational corporations. The emergence of a single world market signals the erosion of state power and legitimacy. Hyperglobalists predict that the Northern hemisphere/Southern hemisphere dichotomy will be supplanted by a global entrepreneurial order governed by economic "rules of the game," such as those codified by the World Trade Organization (WTO). Hyperglobalists accept short-term winners and losers but insist that, in the long run, the rising global tide will eventually lift all national and individual boats—except for those who resist the all-but-inevitable progress promised by globalization. As development economist Dani Rodrik observes, "global integration has become, for all practical purposes, a substitute for a development strategy." Consequently, advocates of this view claim, governmental attention and resources should be directed toward rapid (and often painful) removal of tariffs and other devices that block access to the globalizing world. British prime minister Tony Blair has succinctly expressed the hyperglobalist faith:

> [We] have an enormous job to do to convince the sincere and well-motivated opponents of the WTO agenda that the WTO can be, indeed is, a friend of development, and that far from impoverishing the world's poorer countries, trade liberalization is the only sure route to the kind of economic growth needed to bring their prosperity closer to that of the major developed economies.

Skepticism. The skeptic of globalism's promise offers another interpretation, which takes one of two forms. Skeptics such as international relations theorists Stephen Krassner and Samuel Huntington reject the hyperglobalist view that worldwide economic integration is taking place at all. Krassner argues that regional trading blocks and some national governments are becoming stronger. Huntington contends that resurgent fundamentalist cultures either insulate themselves from or clash with alien cultures (especially those shaped by Western consumerism).

A second brand of skepticism is characterized by the work of economist Herman Daly, who in these pages conceded that hyperglobalist trends exist but argues that states should remain the dominant economic and cultural force. Daly contends that states *should* resist economic openness and instead emphasize national and local well-being. Skeptics such as Daly insist, further, that economic integration, cross-boundary financial investment, the digital revolution, and multinational power do not extinguish the Northern hemisphere/Southern hemisphere divide. To the contrary, poor countries in the South will face even greater poverty because, as Rodrik has argued, poor nations focused on international integration will "divert human resources, administrative capabilities and political capital away from more urgent development priorities such as education, public health, industrial capacity, and social cohesions. This emphasis also undermines nascent democratic institutions by removing the choice of development strategy from public debate."

Transformationalism. A third interpretation, transformationalism, views the phenomenon of globalization as a historically unprecedented and powerful set of processes (with multiple causes) that result in a more interconnected and organizationally multifaceted world. But, contends the transformationalist, it is too simple to say that state power is either eroded or reinforced—it is more accurate to conclude that the nation-state is increasingly reconstituted as part of regional, hemispheric, and global institutions, with some nations gaining and other losing power. In particular, the old Northern hemisphere/ Southern hemisphere dichotomy will be replaced. As Held and his colleagues predict,

> North and South are increasingly becoming meaningless categories: under conditions of globalization distributional patterns of power and wealth no longer accord with a simple core and periphery division of the world, as in the early twentieth century, but reflect a new geography of power and privilege which transcends political borders and regions, reconfiguring established international and transnational hierarchies of social power and wealth.

According to this view, three new distributional patterns will emerge, with some individuals and institutions characterized as "elite," others "contented," and a third group "marginalized."

Transformationalists are both less enthusiastic than hyperglobalists and less pessimistic than skeptics. The globalizing world exhibits neither the intrinsic good that the hyperglobalists celebrate nor the unmitigated evil that the skeptics worry about. Instead, transformationalists insist, globalization at times impedes—but at times enables—good human and communal development.

The Capabilities Approach

Relying on both empirical and normative inquiry, development ethicists should offer ethical appraisals of globalization and make suggestions for better ways of managing new and evolving global interconnectedness. Typically, globalization's uneven, and frequently changing influences on individuals and communities can be understood by empirical disciplines and addressed by policy tools. But it is not enough to inquire how or why globalization affects human choice and institutional distribution. Understanding the significance of globalization's consequences requires application of ethical criteria and a theory of justice.

The most promising approach to the normative dimensions of development ethics and globalization is the capabilities perspective. The development ethicist advocating the capability perspective will scrutinize the effects different kinds of globalization have on *everyone's* capabilities for living lives that are—among other things—long, healthy, secure, autonomous, socially engaged, and politically participatory. Because these valuable capabilities are the basis for human rights and duties, this type of development ethicist also examines how globalization helps or hinders individuals and institutions as they fulfill their moral duties to respect rights. Good national and global development protects, secures, and restores an adequate level of morally basic capabilities for everyone in the world—regardless of nationality, ethnicity, age, gender, or sexual preference. Such global phenomena as worldwide networks of terrorism, money laundering, illegal drug distribution, sex tourism, and forced migrations should be resisted. On the other hand, global dispersion of human rights and democratic norms should be promoted. The ethical status of other aspects of globalization—such as open trade, foreign direct investments, and the growth of multinational corporations—is less clear. The extent to which these elements of globalization enhance, secure, or restore human capabilities will depend on context and especially on how a national polity integrates and shapes global forces.

Although the capabilities approach challenges national and regional communities to promote human capabilities, it also challenges territorial political communities and transnational agencies—the European Union, United Nations, World Trade Organization, World Bank, International Commission of Human Rights, Human Rights Watch, and the ICC, among others—to take responsibility for setting policies that improve the chances of all persons to live decent lives. Further, these overlapping political communities should themselves be civilized and democratized, allowing individuals to exercise such capabilities as political participation and democratic deliberation.

Humanizing and Democratizing Globalization: Three Projects

Development ethicists have identified three projects that respond to the normative challenges presented by globalization. If development ethics has the task, as Goulet once observed, of "keeping hope alive," one way to do so is to identify best practices and promising projects for globalization with a human and democratic face.

Liberal internationalism, one project, expressed in, among other sources, the Commission on Global Governance's *Our Global Neighbourhood,* advocates introduction of democratic practices in those sovereign nation-states and international organizations that lack them. It encourages democratic reform, favorable loan terms and loan forgiveness, and the help of such international judicial institutions such as the recently ratified International Criminal Court (ICC), which will have jurisdiction over war crimes and other violations of internationally recognized human rights. It is anticipated that, with the existence of the ICC, the UN can more effectively express the will of the majority of participating states rather than that of the members of the Security Council.

Radical republicanism, expressed clearly in, for instance, Richard Falk's *On Humane Governance: Toward a New Global Politics,* seeks to weaken—if not dismantle—existing nation-states and international institutions in favor of self-governing *alternative* communities committed to the public good and harmony with the natural environment. Radical republicanism gives priority to those grassroots and indigenous communities that resist globalization in all its forms. This bottom-up approach advocates the use of communications technology to allow diverse grassroots or local groups to become a global "civil society" united by similar concerns and aspirations for action. If radical republicanism succeeds, one can anticipate that institutions such as the World Bank would become obsolete or decentralized, and even institutions such as the ICC, which would be seen as dominated by elites, would be dismantled in favor of national or, better, local judicial processes. The radical republican insists that indigenous communities, regardless whether they are located within only one nation-state, should govern themselves according to their own rules and traditions, and democracy should be largely direct and local and decisions should be made by consensus.

Cosmopolitan democracy rejects both the liberal internationalist's goal of reform and the radical republican's goal of abolition. Instead, the cosmopolitan seeks a kind of global governance that consists in a "double democratization." The first part of double democratization advocates nation-states either initiating or further promoting popular rule, resulting in a decentralization of political power.

The second part of double democratization calls for the promotion of robust public debate and democratic deliberation that extends beyond national boundaries. The cosmopolitan also anticipates that nation-states can come to share sovereignty with transnational bodies of various sorts (regional, intercontinental, and global), and that these bodies themselves would be characterized by democratic control.

Institutional democratization requires crafting new and complex individual moral identities, and a new ideal of multiple citizenship. People would no longer view themselves as nothing more than members of a particular local, ethnic, religious, or national group; instead, they would see themselves as human beings with moral responsibilities to all other humans. One can anticipate that citizenship will become multi-layered and complex—one might come to see oneself as the citizen of a neighborhood, a nation, and also accept cosmopolitan citizenship. The notion of citizenship would take seriously a commitment to human rights, including the right of democratic participation, and the duty to promote human development in all aspects of human organization. As Held and his colleagues contend,

> democracy for the new millennium must allow cosmopolitan citizens to gain access to, mediate between and render accountable the social, economic and political processes and flows that cut across and transform their traditional community boundaries. The core of this project involves reconceiving legitimate political authority in a manner which disconnects it from its traditional anchor in fixed borders and delimited territories and, instead, articulates it as an attribute of basic democratic arrangements or basic democratic law which can, in principle, be entrenched and drawn on in diverse self-regulating associations—from cities and subnational regions, to nation-states, regions and wider global networks.

Although all three political projects emphasize different normative commitments, they all argue that a variety of human organizations can become platforms for democratization. They differ most in their views of how "deep" the democratization can—or must—go and the extent to which the current world order is inimical to democratization and international justice. While liberal internationalists and cosmopolitan democrats share many democratic and participatory values with radical republicans, they judge radical republicans too utopian about grassroots reform and too pessimistic about the democratic potential of national or transnational institutions. The challenges of globalization expand—rather than narrow—the agenda of development ethics. Interdisciplinary and cross-cultural dialogue and forums of democratic deliberation allow development ethicists to understand and secure genuinely human development at all levels of political community and in all kinds of regional and global institutions. As Sen remarks in concluding "How to Judge Globalism,"

> the central issue of contention is not globalization itself, nor is it the use of the market as an institution, but the inequity in the overall balance of institutional arrangements—which produces very unequal sharing of the benefits of globalization. The question is not just whether the poor, too, gain something from globalization, but whether they get a fair share and a fair opportunity. There is an urgent need for reforming institutional arrangements—in addition to national ones—to overcome both the errors of omission and those of commission that tend to give the poor across the world such limited opportunities. Globalization deserves a reasoned defense, but it also needs reform.

This chapter first appeared in *Philosophy & Public Policy Quarterly*, vol. 22, no. 4 (Fall 2002), and is drawn from "Globalization and Human Development: Ethical Approaches," in *Proceedings of the Seventh Plenary Session of the Pontifical Academy of Social Sciences, the Vatican, 25–28 April 2001*, edited by Edmond Malinvaud and Louis Sabourin (Vatican City: Pontifical Academy of the Social Sciences, 2001).

Sources and Annotated Bibliography

World Hunger and Moral Obligation, edited by W. Aiken and H. LaFollette (Prentice Hall, 1976) (expands material on philosophical debates in the early seventies over the ethics of food aid); *World Hunger and Morality*, edited by W. Aiken and H. LaFollette (Prentice Hall, 1996, second edition) (expands material on the philosophical recasting of ethics of food aid to an ethics of development and international justice); D. Archibugi, D. Held, and Martin Kóhler, *Re-imagining Political Community: Studies in Cosmopolitan Democracy* (Stanford University Press, 1998) (a collection of essays advocating transformationalism and cosmopolitan democracy); *International Justice and the Third World*, edited by R. Attfield and B. Wilkins (Routledge, 1992) (British essays on development ethics and international justice); P. Berger, *Pyramids of Sacrifice: Political Ethics and Social Change* (Basic Books, 1974) (challenging essay linking "political ethics" and Third World poverty); L. Camacho, *Ciencia y tecnolo-*

gia en el subdesarrollo (Editorial Tecnológica de Costa Rica, 1993) (leading Latin American philosopher of development and technology); *Our Global Neighborhood,* a publication of the Commission on Global Governance (Oxford University Press, 1995) (defends a liberal-internationalist project for humanizing globalization); D. A. Crocker, *Florecimiento humano y desarrollo internacional: La nueva ética de capacidades* (Editorial de la Universidad de Costa Rica, 1998) (an analysis and positive assessment of the ethical foundations of Sen and Nussbaum's capability approach); D. A. Crocker, "Toward Development Ethics," *World Development* 19 (1991) (an introductory survey and bibliography of the nature, methods, and value of development ethics); D. A. Crocker, Luis Camacho, and Ramón Romero, "Globalization, Consumption Patterns, and Human Development: The Cases of Costa Rica and Honduras," background paper for *United Nations Development Programme, Human Development Report,* 1998 (an application of a version of the capabilities approach to assess the impact on human development of globalization and especially Northern consumption norms in two Central American countries); Herman E. Daly, "Globalization and Its Discontents," *Philosophy & Public Policy Quarterly,* vol. 21, no. 2/3 (2001); N. Dower, "What Is Development?—A Philosopher's Answer," *Centre for Development Studies Occasional Paper Series,* 3 (University of Glasgow, 1988) (argues for the role of philosophers in development studies and for the normative meaning of "development" as "a process of socio-economic change which ought to take place"); N. Dower, *World Ethics: The New Agenda* (Edinburgh University Press, 1998) (a leading development ethicist addresses development in the context of international relations and a "world ethic"); *Ethics of Environment and Development: Global Challenge, International Response,* edited by J. R. Engel and J. G. Engel (University of Arizona Press, 1990) (an international collection that explores different ways of relating environmental and development ethics); A. Escobar, *Encountering Development: The Making and Unmaking of the Third World* (Princeton University Press, 1995) (postmodernist "deconstruction" of development theory and practice as imperialist and destructive of traditional life); R. Falk, *On Humane Governance: Toward a New Global Politics* (Polity Press, 1995) (this international law scholar defends a radical republican project for humanizing globalization); T. L. Friedman, *The Lexus and the Olive Tree: Understanding Globalization* (Farrar, Straus & Giroux, 1999) (a popular defense of hyperglobalism); D. Gasper, "Development Ethics: An Emergent Field?" in *Market Forces and World Development,* edited by R. Prendergast and F. Stewart (St. Martin's Press, 1994) (a helpful stocktaking that defends development ethics as a "multidisciplinary field" that closes the gap between abstract philosophy and practical experience in order to promote desirable change in poor countries);

D. Goulet, *The Cruel Choice: A New Concept in the Theory of Development* (Athenaeum, 1971) (the classic text by a development ethics pioneer); D. Goulet, *Development Ethics: A Guide to Theory and Practice* (Zed, 1995) (a collection of Goulet's articles since 1971 with some new essays); *Ethical Dilemmas of Development in Asia*, edited by G. Gunatilleke, N. Tiruchelvam, and R. Coomaraswamy (Lexington Books, 1988) (accessible international collection addressing ethical, empirical, and political aspects of Asian development); D. Held, A. McGrew, D. Goldblatt, and J. Perraton, *Global Transformations* (Stanford University Press, 1999) (a helpful analysis and assessment of three approaches to globalization—hyperglobalism, skepticism, and transformationalism—and an important effort to defend the latter as a systematic theory of globalization). To complement the informal definition of "globalization," David Held and his colleagues more formally characterize globalization as "a process (or set of processes) which embodies a transformation in the spatial organization of social relations and transactions—assessed in terms of their extensity, intensity, velocity and impact—generation of transcontinental or interregional flows and networks of activity, interaction, and the exercise of power." P. Hirst and G. Thompson, *Globalization in Question: The International Economy and the Possibilities of Governance* (Polity Press, 1996) (a skeptical critique of globalization, arguing that globalization is a myth that masks the continuing role of powerful nation-states advancing their interests through regional trading blocks); S. P. Huntington, *The Clash of Civilizations and the Remaking of the World Order* (Simon and Schuster, 1996) (a critic of hyperglobalism, this skeptic argues that the world is fragmenting and clashing along cultural and religious fault lines); B. Kliksberg, "El rol del capital social y de la cultura en el proceso de desarrollo," in *Capital social y culura: Claves Estratégicas para el desarrollo*, edited by B. Kliksberg and L. Tomassini (Banco Inter-americana de Desarrollo, 2000) (an important essay arguing that "social capital" is both an end in itself and means to genuine development); *Global Sustainable Development in the 21st Century*, edited by K. Lee, A. Holland, and D. McNeill (Edinburgh University Press, 2000) (a recent collection that probes the concept of sustainable development as a way of balancing conservation and development); M. Nussbaum, *Women and Human Development: The Capabilities Approach* (Cambridge University Press, 2000) (Nussbaum's most important statement of her version of the capabilities approach applied to women's deprivations and opportunities); *Women, Culture and Development*, edited by M. Nussbaum and J. Glover (Clarendon Press, 1995) (a valuable international collection of advanced essays explaining, assessing, and applying the capabilities ethic to the issue of gender equality in developing countries); *The Quality of Life*, edited by M. Nussbaum and A. Sen (Clarendon

Press, 1993) (advanced essays that clarify and evaluate the capabilities and other approaches to quality of life in both rich and poor countries); K. Ohmae, *The End of the Nation State* (Free Press, 1995) (this volume defends a hyperglobalist approach to globalization); O. O'Neill, "Ending World Hunger," in *Matters of Life and Death*, edited by T. Regan (Allen & Unwin, 1993) (a critique of utilitarian approaches to world hunger and an accessible statement of the author's Kantian duty-based ethic of aid and development); O. O'Neill, *Faces of Hunger: An Essay on Poverty, Justice and Development* (Allen & Unwin, 1986) (O'Neill's Kantian refocusing of the ethical challenge from aid to development); D. Rodrik, "Trading in Illusions," *Foreign Policy* (March/April 2000) (a trenchant critique of hyperglobalism's claims that global economic integration causes economic growth and democratization in poor nations); J. M. Segal, "What Is Development?" in *Philosophical Dimensions of Public Policy*, edited by Verna V. Gehring and William A. Galston (Transaction Publishers, 2002) (first appearing in the mideighties, this influential paper argues for an ethically based concept of development and evaluates three development models: growth, growth with equity, and basic needs); A. Sen, *Resources, Values and Development* (Harvard University Press, 1984) (contains several of Sen's important early papers on the capabilities approach to development); A. Sen, "Development Thinking at the Beginning of the 21st Century," in *Economic and Social Development into the XXI Century*, edited by Louis Emmerij (Inter-American Development Bank, 1997); A. Sen, *Development as Freedom* (Knopf, 1999) (Sen's most recent and accessible articulation of his agency-centered capabilities approach); A. Sen and J. Drèze, *Hunger and Public Action* (Oxford University Press, 1989) (an application of the capabilities approach—its normative foundations and policy implications—to famine and chronic malnutrition in poor countries); A. Sen, "How to Judge Globalism," *American Prospect* (Winter 2002); P. Streeten, P. with S. J. Burki, M. Haq, N. Hicks, and F. Stewart, *First Things First: Meeting Basic Needs in Developing Countries* (Oxford, 1981) (the classic statement of the basic-needs approach to change in poor countries); United Nations Development Programme, *Human Development Report* (Oxford University Press, 1998, 1999, 2000) (these three UNDP reports operationalize the capabilities approach to appraise, respectively, consumption, globalization, and human rights).

Globalization and Its Discontents

Herman E. Daly

Every day, newspaper articles and television reports insist that those who oppose globalization must be isolationists or—even worse—xenophobes. This judgment is nonsense. The relevant alternative to globalization is internationalization, which is neither isolationist nor xenophobic. Yet it is impossible to recognize the cogency of this alternative if one does not properly distinguish these two terms.

"Internationalization" refers to the increasing importance of relations among nations. Although the basic unit of community and policy remains the nation, increasingly trade, treaties, alliances, protocols, and other formal agreements and communications are necessary elements for nations to thrive. "Globalization" refers to global economic integration of many formerly national economies into one global economy. Economic integration is made possible by free trade—especially by free capital mobility—and by easy or uncontrolled migration. In contrast to internationalization, which simply recognizes that nations increasingly rely on understandings among one another, globalization is the effective erasure of national boundaries for economic purposes. National boundaries become totally porous with respect to goods and capital, and ever more porous with respect to people, who are simply viewed as cheap labor—or in some cases as cheap human capital.

In short, globalization is the economic integration of the globe. But exactly what is "integration"? The word derives from *integer,* meaning one, complete, or whole. Integration means much more than "interdependence"—it is the act of combining separate although related units into a single whole. Since there can be only one whole, only one unity with reference to which parts are integrated, it follows that global economic integration logically implies national economic *dis*integration—parts are torn out of their national context (dis-integrated), in order to be re-integrated into the new whole, the globalized economy.

As the saying goes, to make an omelet you have to break some eggs. The disintegration of the national egg is necessary to integrate the global omelet. But this obvious logic, as well as the cost of disintegration, is frequently met with denial. This chapter argues that globalization is neither inevitable nor to be embraced, much less celebrated. Acceptance of globalization entails several serious consequences, namely, standards-lowering competition, an increased tolerance of mergers and monopoly power, intense national specialization, and the excessive monopolization of knowledge as "intellectual property." This chapter discusses these likely consequences, and concludes by advocating the adoption of internationalization, and not globalization.

The Inevitability of Globalization?

Some accept the inevitability of globalization and encourage others in the faith. With admirable clarity, honesty, and brevity, Renato Ruggiero, former director-general of the World Trade Organization, insists that "we are no longer writing the rules of interaction among separate national economies. We are writing the constitution of a single global economy." His sentiments clearly affirm globalization and reject internationalization as above defined. Further, those who hold Ruggiero's view also subvert the charter of the Bretton Woods institutions. Named after a New Hampshire resort where representatives of forty-four nations met in 1944 to design the world's post-World War II economic order, the institutions conceived at the Bretton Woods International Monetary Conference include the World Bank and the International Monetary Fund. The World Trade Organization evolved later but functions as a third sister to the World Bank and the International Monetary Fund. The nations at the conference considered proposals by the US, U.K., and Canadian governments, and developed the "Bretton Woods system," which established a stable international environment through such policies as fixed exchange rates, currency convertibility, and provision for orderly exchange-rate adjustments. The Bretton Woods Institutions were designed to facilitate *internationalization, not globalization*, a point ignored by director-general Ruggiero.

The World Bank, along with its sister institutions, seems to have lost sight of its mission. After the disruption of its meetings in Washington, D.C., in April 2000, the World Bank sponsored an Internet discussion on globalization. The closest the World Bank came to offering a definition of the subject under discussion was the following: "The most common core sense of economic globalization . . . surely refers to the observation that in recent years a quickly rising share of economic activity in the world seems to be taking place between people who live in different countries (rather than in the same country)." This ambiguous description was not improved upon by Mr. Wolfensohn, president of the World Bank, who told the audience at a subsequent Aspen Institute conference that "globalization is a practical methodology for empowering the poor to improve their lives." That is neither a definition nor a description—it is a wish. Further, this wish also flies in the face of the real consequences of global economic integration. One could only sympathize with demonstrators protesting Mr. Wolfensohn's speech some fifty yards from the Aspen conference facility. The reaction of the Aspen elite was to accept as truth the title of Mr. Wolfensohn's speech, "Making Globalization Work for the Poor," and then ask in grieved tones, "How could anyone demonstrate against *that?*"

Serious consequences flow from the World Bank's lack of precision in defining globalization but lauding it nonetheless. For one thing, the so-called definition of globalization conflates the concept with that of internationalization. As a result, one cannot reasonably address a crucial question: Should these increasing transactions between people living in different countries take place *across national boundaries* that are economically significant, or *within an integrated world* in which national boundaries are economically meaningless?

The ambiguous understanding of globalization deprives citizens of the opportunity to decide whether they are willing to abandon national monetary and fiscal policy, as well as the minimum wage. One also fails to carefully consider whether economic integration entails political and cultural integration. In short, will political communities and cultural traditions wither away, subsumed under some monolithic economic imperative? Although one might suspect economic integration would lead to political integration, it is hard to decide which would be worse—an economically integrated world *with*, or *without*, political integration. Everyone recognizes the desirability of community for the world as a whole—but one can conceive of two very different models of world community: (1) a federated community of real national communities (internationalization) versus (2) a cosmopolitan direct membership in a single abstract global community (globalization). However, at present our confused conversations about globalization deprive us of the opportunity to reflect deeply on these very different possibilities.

This chapter has suggested that at present organizations such as the International Monetary Fund and the World Bank (and, by extension, the World Trade Organization) no longer serve the interests of their member nations as defined in their charters. Yet if one asks whose interests are served, we are told they service the interests of the integrated "global economy." If one tries to glimpse a concrete reality behind that grand abstraction, however, one can find no individual workers, peasants, or small businessmen represented, but only giant fictitious individuals, the transnational corporations. In globalization, power is drained away from national communities and local enterprises, and aggregates in transnational corporations.

The Consequences of Globalization

Globalization—the erasure of national boundaries for economic purposes—risks serious consequences. Briefly, they include, first of all, standards-lowering competition to externalize social and environmental costs with the goal of achievement of a competitive advantage. This results, in effect, in a race to the bottom so far as efficiency in cost accounting and equity in income distribution are concerned. Globalization also risks increased tolerance of mergers and monopoly power in domestic markets in order that corporations become big enough to compete internationally. Third, globalization risks more intense national specialization according to the dictates of competitive advantage. Such specialization reduces the range of choice of ways to earn a livelihood, and increases dependence on other countries. Finally, worldwide enforcement of a muddled and self-serving doctrine of "trade-related intellectual property rights" is a direct contradiction of the Jeffersonian dictum that "knowledge is the common property of mankind."

Each of these risks of globalization deserves closer scrutiny.

Standards-lowering competition. Globalization undercuts the ability of nations to internalize environmental and social costs into prices. Instead, economic integration under free market conditions promotes standards-lowering competition—a race to the bottom, in short. The country that does the poorest job of internalizing all social and environmental costs of production into its prices gets a competitive advantage in international trade. The external social and environmental costs are left to be borne by the population at large. Further, more of world production shifts to countries that do the poorest job of counting costs—a sure recipe for reducing the efficiency of global production.

As uncounted, externalized costs increase, the positive correlation between gross domestic product (GDP) growth and welfare disappears, or even becomes negative. We enter a world foreseen by the nineteenth-century social critic John Ruskin, who observed that "that which seems to be wealth is in verity but a gilded index of far-reaching ruin."

Another dimension of the race to the bottom is that globalization fosters increasing inequality in the distribution of income in high-wage countries, such as the US. Historically, in the US there has been an implicit social contract established to ameliorate industrial strife between labor and capital. As a consequence, the distribution of income between labor and capital has been considered more equal and just in the US compared to the world as a whole. However, global integration of markets necessarily abrogates that social contract. US wages would fall drastically because labor is relatively more abundant globally than nationally. Further, returns to capital in the US would increase because capital is relatively more scarce globally than nationally. Although one could make the theoretical argument that wages would be bid up in the rest of the world, the increase would be so small as to be insignificant. Making such an argument from the relative numbers would be analogous to insisting that, theoretically, when I jump off a ladder gravity not only pulls me to the earth but also moves the earth toward me. This technical point offers cold comfort to anyone seeking a softer landing.

Increased tolerance of mergers and monopoly power. Fostering global competitive advantage is used as an excuse for tolerance of corporate mergers and monopoly in national markets. Chicago School economist and Nobel laureate Ronald Coase, in his classic article on the theory of the firm, suggests that corporate entities are "islands of central planning in a sea of market relationships." The islands of central planning become larger and larger relative to the remaining sea of market relationships as a result of merger. More and more resources are allocated by within-firm central planning and less by between-firm market relationships. Corporations are the victor, and the market principle is the loser, as governments lose the strength to regulate corporate capital and maintain competitive markets in the public interest. Of the hundred largest economic organizations, fifty-two are corporations and forty-eight are nations. The distribution of income within these centrally-planned corporations has become much more concentrated. The ratio of the salary of the Chief Executive Officer to the average employee has passed 400 (as one would expect, since chief central planners set their own salaries).

Intense national specialization. Free trade and free capital mobility increase pressures for specialization in order to gain or maintain a competitive advantage. As a consequence, globalization demands that workers accept an ever-narrowing range of ways to earn a livelihood. In Uruguay, for example, everyone would have to be either a shepherd or a cowboy to conform to the dictates of competitive advantage in the global market. Everything else should be imported in exchange for beef, mutton, wool, and leather. Any Uruguayan who wants to play in a symphony orchestra or be an airline pilot should emigrate.

Of course, most people derive as much satisfaction from how they earn their income as from how they spend it. Narrowing that range of choice is a welfare loss uncounted by trade theorists. Globalization assumes either that emigration and immigration are costless, or that narrowing the range of occupational choice within a nation is costless. Both assumptions are false.

While trade theorists ignore the range of choice in *earning* one's income, they at the same time exaggerate the welfare effects of range of choice in *spending* that income. For example, the US imports Danish butter cookies and Denmark imports US butter cookies.

Although the gains from trading such similar commodities cannot be great, trade theorists insist that the welfare of cookie connoisseurs is increased by expanding the range of consumer choice to the limit.

Perhaps, but one wonders whether those gains might be realized more cheaply by simply trading recipes. Although one would think so, recipes—trade-related intellectual property rights—are the one thing that free traders really want to protect.

Intellectual property rights. Of all things, knowledge is that which should be most freely shared, since in sharing, knowledge is multiplied rather than divided. Yet trade theorists have rejected Thomas Jefferson's dictum that "knowledge is the common property of mankind" and instead have accepted a muddled doctrine of "trade-related intellectual property rights." This notion of rights grants private corporations monopoly ownership of the very basis of life itself—patents to seeds (including the patent-protecting, life-denying terminator gene) and to knowledge of basic genetic structures.

The argument offered to support this grab is that, without the economic incentive of monopoly ownership, little new knowledge and innovation will be forthcoming. Yet, so far as I know, James Watson and Francis Crick, co-discoverers of the structure of DNA, do not share in the patent royalties reaped by their successors. Nor of course did Gregor Mendel get any royalties—but then he was a monk motivated by mere curiosity about how Creation works!

Once knowledge exists, its proper price is the marginal opportunity cost of sharing it, which is close to zero, since nothing is lost by sharing knowledge. Of course, one does lose the monopoly on that knowledge, but then economists have traditionally argued that *monopoly* is inefficient as well as unjust because it creates an artificial scarcity of the monopolized item.

Certainly, the cost of production of new knowledge is not zero, even though the cost of sharing it is. This allows biotech corporations to claim that they deserve a fifteen- or twenty-year monopoly for the expenses incurred in research and development. Although corporations deserve to profit from their efforts, they are not entitled to monopolize on Watson and Crick's contribution—without which they could do nothing—or on the contributions of Gregor Mendel and all the great scientists of the past who made fundamental discoveries. As early twentieth-century economist Joseph Schumpeter emphasized, being the first with an innovation already gives one the advantage of novelty, a natural temporary monopoly, which in his view was the major source of profit in a competitive economy.

As the great Swiss economist, Jean Sismondi, argued over two centuries ago, not all new knowledge is of benefit to humankind.

We need a sieve to select beneficial knowledge. Perhaps the worse selective principle is hope for private monetary gain. A much better selective motive for knowledge is a search in hopes of benefit to our fellows. This is not to say that we should abolish all intellectual property rights—that would create more problems than it would solve. But we should certainly begin restricting the domain and length of patent monopolies rather than increasing them so rapidly and recklessly. We should also become much more willing to share knowledge. Shared knowledge increases the productivity of all labor, capital, and resources. Further, international development aid should consist far more of freely shared knowledge, and far less of foreign investment and interest-bearing loans.

Let me close with my favorite quote from John Maynard Keynes, one of the founders of the recently subverted Bretton Woods Institutions:

> I sympathize therefore, with those who would minimize, rather than those who would maximize, economic entanglement between nations. Ideas, knowledge, art, hospitality, travel—these are the things which should of their nature be international. But let goods be homespun whenever it is reasonably and conveniently possible; and, above all, let finance be primarily national.

This chapter appeared previously in *Philosophy & Public Policy Quarterly*, vol. 21, no. 2/3 (Spring/Summer 2001), and arose from a discussion given at the Aspen Institute's 50th Anniversary Conference, "Globalization and the Human Condition," held in Aspen, Colorado, on August 20, 2000.

Globalization's Major Inconsistencies

Herman E. Daly

Advocates of globalization want goods, services, and capital to flow without restriction across national boundaries. They contend that global gains are made from free trade. But what about the free migration of people? The same economic logic of global gains from trade applies with equal force to free movement of labor (or human capital). Globalization and free trade advocates, along with such powerful organizations as the World Trade Organization (WTO), the International Bank for Reconstruction and Development (IBRD), and the International Monetary Fund (IMF), all support the free flow of goods, services, and capital. Yet they do not support the free migration of people.

Although *people* do not migrate freely, many jobs do. Recently, for instance, the task of writing welfare checks to New Jersey's unemployed was "outsourced" to India, prompting an alert politician to publicly wonder whether at least some unemployed citizens of New Jersey could not be employed writing welfare checks to remaining unemployed citizens. But such common sense is ruled out by the reality of low wages in India and the "logic" of global efficiency. This "logic" is mistakenly held by many free trade advocates to derive from eighteenth-century economist David Ricardo's theory of comparative advantage. The purpose of this chapter is to examine why the view of free trade advocates and some supporters of globalization is mistaken. One can usefully begin by recalling several essential elements of the view of comparative advantage to see the mistaken logic of one aspect of efficiency.

Absolute versus Comparative Advantage

Briefly, a country has an *absolute* advantage in producing a good if it can produce that good with less labor and capital per unit than can other countries. A country has a *comparative* advantage if it can produce that good more cheaply (with less labor and capital) relative to other goods than is the case in other countries. In the first case one compares absolute costs *across* countries; in the second case one compares absolute costs *within* each country and compares ratios of internal national costs between countries. Ricardo showed that countries can mutually benefit from free trade so long as their internal cost ratios differ, regardless of absolute cost differences. This is considered by some to be the "deepest and most beautiful result in all of economics." As a result, according to this view, capital and labor should be devoted in each country to producing those goods that are relatively cheapest for it to produce, and a country should trade for those goods that are relatively more expensive to produce internally. However, if capital (and labor) can cross borders to pursue *absolutely* lower cost, then the whole reason-to-be for comparative advantage as a clever adaptation to the constraint of internationally immobile capital and labor completely disappears!

The question thus arises: why constrain labor; that is, why prevent people from moving as free economic actors in the new, global economy? One reason for the restraint on migration has much to do with the fact that placing constraints on the mobility of a factor of production puts that factor at a competitive disadvantage in the distributive struggle. Because capital is more mobile than labor, capital has more options, increasing its bargaining power in wage negotiations. Companies threaten to move to another country—an easy transfer of capital—and workers relinquish their wage demands because it is impossible for them to move as well. Further, since the WTO, IBRD, and IMF are friendlier to capital than to labor, they promote the international mobility of capital but not of labor. (*The Wall Street Journal*, typically friendly to capital interests, surprisingly yet consistently favors free migration of labor. However, when one looks closer, perhaps what the *Journal* actually favors is free immigration of *cheap* labor into the US.)

The Free Trader's Misgivings about Open Migration

At a deeper level, free trade advocates perhaps recoil from free migration because they can see that it would lead to massive relocation of people between world regions of vastly differing wealth, creating a tragedy of the open access commons. The strain on local communities, both the sending and the receiving, would be enormous. In the face of unlimited migration, they might ask, how could any national community maintain a minimum wage, a welfare program, subsidized medical care, or a public school system? How could a nation punish its criminals and tax evaders if workers were free to emigrate? Indeed, one wonders, would it not be much cheaper to encourage emigration of a country's poor, sick, or criminals, rather than run welfare programs, charity hospitals, and prisons? (Fidel Castro took precisely this course of action in opening Cuba's jails in 1980. His policy encouraged a mass migration of prisoners and others that became part of the wave of "marielito" immigrants to the US.) Further, one might reasonably wonder how a country could reap the benefit of educational investments made in its own citizens if those citizens are free to emigrate. Would nations continue to make such investments in the face of free migration and a continuing "brain drain"? Would a country make investments in education if it experienced massive immigration pressures, which would dilute the educational resources of the nation? Would any country any longer try to limit its birth rate, since children who migrate abroad and send back remittances can be a good investment, a fact that might increase the birth rate? (With unfettered migration, a country could never control its numbers anyway.)

Few would deny that some migration is a very good thing—but this discussion concerns *free* migration, where "free" means *deregulated, uncontrolled, unlimited*, as in "free" trade or "free" capital mobility. One must also be mindful that immigrants are people, frequently disadvantaged people. It is a terrible thing to be "anti-immigrant." Free migration is a policy, and one can be *"anti-immigration,"* or more accurately "pro-immigration limits" without in the least being *anti-immigrant*. One kind of globalization advocate, the global cosmopolitan, thinks that it is immoral to make any policy distinction between citizen and noncitizen and therefore favors free migration. Global cosmopolitans also suggest that free migration is the shortest route to their vision of the *summum bonum*, equality of wages worldwide.

Their point is fair enough—there is some logic in their position, so long as the global cosmopolitan is willing to see wages equalized at a *low* level. But those who support free migration as the shortest route to equality of wages worldwide could only with great difficulty try to contend with problems of an open-access commons, and the worry of the destruction of the existing local culture and economy, and other issues raised in the preceding paragraph.

A more workable moral guide is the recognition that one's obligation to noncitizens is to do them no harm, while one's obligation to fellow citizens is *first* to do no harm, and *then* try to do positive good. The many dire consequences of globalization—such as over-specialization in a few volatile export commodities (petroleum, timber, minerals, and other extractive goods with little value added locally, for instance), crushing debt burdens, exchange rate risks and speculative currency destabilization, foreign corporate control of national markets, unnecessary monopolization of "trade-related intellectual property rights" (typically patents on prescription drugs), and not least, easy immigration in the interests of lower wages and cheaper exports—amply show that the "do no harm" criterion is still far from being met.

The Erasure of Economic Policy?

If globalization and free trade advocates refuse to accept that their own view entails embracing free migration, then perhaps they might consider whether their reluctance has a solid basis. They might ask themselves if some of their misgivings about the free flow of people might also apply to the free flow of those elements that are vital to people, especially capital, but also goods and services. Markets abhor boundaries, but public policy in the interest of community *requires* boundaries. Markets require policy and laws for their functioning, so indirectly even markets ultimately require boundaries.

Since globalization is the erasure of national borders for economic purposes, it also comes close to being the erasure of national economic policy as well. In addition, globalization even implies the erasure of international economic policy. For example, suppose all nations agreed to the Kyoto Accord on Global Warming. Now try to imagine how these nations could enforce domestically what they had agreed to internationally if they have no control over their borders. Institutions of control would have to be global because the unit being controlled would be global. And "global" is not to be understood in the federated sense of cooperation among individual nations that control their borders but in the cosmopolitan sense of formerly separate economies now integrated into a single borderless world economy. The strength of global integration might be expressed in the following analogy: International interdependence is to global integration as friendship is to marriage. All nations must be friends, but they probably should not attempt multilateral marriage.

Opposing *free* trade does not necessarily entail supporting *no* trade at all in a world of self-sufficient nations. The opposite of *free* trade is not no trade, it is *regulated* trade. Rather, one reasonably can advocate for *regulated* trade, which is certainly the historical norm. The term "free trade" has become a rhetorically persuasive label for deregulated trade. No one is against freedom, or against trade, but many are against the total deregulation of international commerce. Consider recent examples: Was deregulation of the savings and loan banks such a good idea? Has deregulation of financial markets, stock markets, and energy markets been such a success? Given these fiascos, one wonders why the traditional regulation of international commerce in the national interest has become anathema to most economists. Do they want to abolish the nation and institute a world government? Perhaps they want to create a global open-access commons for corporations to competitively plunder? Given the arrogance and closed mindedness of the free trade establishment it is understandable that the streets of Seattle, and subsequent venues of WTO meetings, have become battlegrounds.

The recent breakdown of WTO talks in Cancun, Mexico, lamented by many, was nevertheless encouraging to others—people are waking up! One source of the breakdown was the absurd, yet long standing, practice of the US and Europe to insist to developing nations that they should practice free trade policies, while the US and Europe massively subsidize their own agricultural concerns. Such subsidies ruin farmers of the developing world and deny them any hope of even relative food self-sufficiency. Developing nations might reasonably respond by enacting countervailing tariffs on agricultural imports, thereby protecting their own agriculture (i.e., negating the advantage of the US and European domestic subsidies). Subsequently, developing countries might negotiate reductions in import tariffs for corresponding reductions in export subsidies. But one sees none of these innovations because the developing world too is entranced by the global model of export-led growth rather than import substitution. They seem to prefer expending their efforts in forcing open the markets of other countries rather than in developing their own internal markets under legitimate protection. Developing internal markets requires a broader distribution of income as well as temporary protection for nascent industries. These are politically difficult measures and are also often opposed by the IMF. "Protection" is considered a pejorative among trade economists, but when pressed on their inconsistency—why they do not favor the "invigorating competition" of free migration—free trade advocates resort to some form of protectionist argument. Yet historically one sees that all developed countries have resorted to protection, most obviously of infant industries and of agriculture.

Comparative Advantage Misapplied

Advocates of globalization and free trade inconsistently hold that migration of labor should not be free. The inconsistency is important, but there exists a crucial subtlety that requires clarification. Once one extends the traditional comparative advantage argument for free trade in goods and services to free trade in capital, then one must realize that it is inconsistent not to apply the comparative advantage argument to other factors, such as labor, as well. But here is the question: Was the first extension, from goods to factors such as capital, legitimate in the first place? The answer is no, since within the context of the traditional comparative advantage argument for free trade, the argument explicitly accepts as a premise the immobility of capital between countries! Both labor and capital must stay at home for Ricardo's comparative advantage argument for free trade to work. If capital and labor, as well as goods and services, are free to move between trading units then we are in the realm of interregional trade, not international trade. For interregional trade the operative principle is absolute advantage, not comparative advantage. If different countries are integrated—that is, they allow for the free flow of capital and labor—they essentially become different regions of the same "country" and comparative advantage gives way to absolute advantage.

One may certainly make a reasonable argument for free trade and specialization in a world of capital mobility and absolute advantage. Alternatively, if one wishes to keep the world safe for comparative advantage and free trade in goods, one must also argue for immobile capital and labor. Yet today's free trade advocates base their case on comparative advantage without being willing to accept the necessary premise of capital immobility. They reason that if free trade in goods is beneficial, then adding free trade in capital just makes it all the more beneficial. However, this view is contrary both to Ricardo and, one might add, logical argumentation, since one cannot use the conclusion of an argument to deny one of its premises.

Further, the reason free traders do not make the free trade case in terms of absolute advantage is because they then would lose the theoretical guarantee that *each* nation is better off as a result of free trade. Under absolute advantage, free trade does not necessarily benefit both partners, although it does benefit the world as a whole in net terms; under comparative advantage free trade does benefit both partners, although not equally. Now one can begin to understand the attitude not just of free trade advocates but of organizations such as the WTO, IMF, and IBRD. The mutual benefit of free trade is a trump card that these advocates and organizations do not want to give up. Without that trump card they would have to face the political question of distribution of these global gains, and they would have to explicitly acknowledge that some countries could lose from free trade.

Who Benefits?

Unwillingness to face this issue is ultimately what led to the failure of the Cancun talks. The South has come to suspect that it is a net loser under the de facto absolute advantage regime of globalization, while the North hides behind the irrelevant theoretical truth that in a comparative advantage regime free trade must necessarily benefit both parties. The theoretical truth is rendered irrelevant by the globalization advocates' insistence on free capital mobility, thereby negating a fundamental premise of comparative advantage. The free trade view chooses to see some aspects of trade and ignore others. They consider only the global sum of individual gains from trade, but they ignore how these gains (and losses) are distributed among individuals or communities, even national communities.

In theory, global gains are even greater under absolute advantage than under comparative advantage because the former removes the constraint of factor immobility. The absolute advantage argument is also considered a very high-minded position, untainted by the sordid vestiges of "nationalism" logically required for comparative advantage. However, if free trade advocates such as the WTO, IMF, and IBRD too explicitly proclaim their globally individualistic cosmopolitan view that only global net gains from trade matter—not *how* gains and losses are distributed among nations—then they are left with an important and problematic consideration.

Consider the IMF, which is a federation of members and which exists to serve the interests of its members. But the IMP's members are *nations*, not individuals, not cosmopolitan, global individuals, and not even transnational corporate "individuals." By vigorously promoting globalization, the IMF has long subverted the independence of its member countries, serving instead the vision of a cosmopolitan, globalized, integrated world economy, rather than the vision of its charter—a federation of nations cooperating as sovereign units to advance the *national* interests of all members.

Working contrary to its charter, the IMF promotes integration at the global level but at the cost of disintegration at the national level. As the old saying goes, to make an omelet, you have to break some eggs. And to carry the analogy forward, one might say that to integrate the global omelet you have to dis-integrate the national eggs. This is the agenda adopted by the IMF, aided by the WTO and the World Bank. Certainly, the IMF should explain to its member countries that their interests as nations are no longer of concern to the cosmopolitan world citizens who run the IMP. One can reasonably wonder, if the IMF no longer serves the interests of its member nations, then whose interests is it serving? This was the tacit question raised to the IMF's partner, the WTO, in Cancun. The developing South, and many in the developed North, would have preferred an answer rather than the evasions they received. Rest assured that question and others raised in this present discussion will be present at the next WTO meeting, along with protesters in the streets.

This chapter first appeared in *Philosophy & Public Policy Quarterly*, vol. 23, no. 4 (Fall 2003).

Sources

The description of Ricardo's result as the "deepest and most beautiful result in all of economics" occurs in R. Findlay, *The World of Economics* (The New Palgrave, 1991), p. 99; for further discussion of the economist Ricardo and his insights, see H. Daly and J. Cobb, *For the Common Good* (Beacon Press, 1994), chapter 11.

Index

About the Editor and Contributors

David A. Crocker is senior research scholar at the Institute for Philosophy and Public Policy and the School of Public Policy at the University of Maryland. He specializes in applied ethics and sociopolitical philosophy, international development ethics, transitional justice, democracy and democratization, and the ethics of consumption. He is faculty advisor for the school's Development Circle, associate director of its Ph.D. program, and teaches in the Maryland Leadership Institute, a summer program for minority undergraduate students seeking careers in public policy and international affairs. In the school's new development program, he teaches courses on ethics, development, foreign aid, democracy, and human rights. Crocker has taught philosophy for twenty-five years at Colorado State University and has been a visiting professor at the University of Munich and twice a Fulbright Scholar at the University of Costa Rica. Crocker is a founder and former president of the International Development Ethics Association (IDEA), an association of scholars and practitioners who apply ethical reflection to development institutions and policies. In the fall of 2005, he held the UNESCO chair in the Department of Philosophy at the University of Valencia, Spain. He is former chair of the American Philosophical Association's Committee on International Cooperation and currently a member of the Executive Council of the Human Development and Capability Association. Among his publications are *Praxis and Democratic Socialism* (1983); editor of (with

Toby Linden) *Ethics of Consumption: The Good Life, Justice, and Global Stewardship* (1998); *Florecimiento humano y desarrollo internacional: La nueva ética de capacidades humanas* (1998); editor of (with Jesus Conill) *¿Republicanismo y educación cívica: Más allá del liberalismo?* (2003); and the forthcoming *The Ethics of Global Development: Agency, Capability, and Deliberative Democracy.*

Herman E. Daly came to the School of Public Policy, the University of Maryland, from the World Bank, where he was senior economist in the Environment Department, helping to develop policy guidelines related to sustainable development. While there, he was engaged in environmental operations work in Latin America. Before joining the World Bank, Daly was alumni professor of economics at Louisiana State University. He is a cofounder and associate editor of the journal *Ecological Economics.* His interest in economic development, population, resources, and environment has resulted in over a hundred articles as well as numerous books, including *Steady-State Economics* (1977; 1991), *Valuing the Earth* (1993), *Beyond Growth* (1996), and *Ecological Economics and the Ecology of Economics* (1999). He is coauthor with theologian John B. Cobb Jr. of *For the Common Good* (1989; 1994), which received the Grawemeyer Award for ideas for improving World Order. He is a recipient of the Honorary Right Livelihood Award (Sweden's alternative to the Nobel Prize), the Heineken Prize for Environmental Science, from the Royal Netherlands Academy of Arts and Sciences, and the Sophie Prize (Norway).

Stephen L. Esquith has been professor and chair of the Department of Philosophy at the Michigan State University but will return from a Fulbright Fellowship year in Mali to take up responsibilities as dean of a new residential college in the arts and humanities that will have a special focus on art and culture, globalization, international ethics, world languages, and civic engagement at Michigan State University. Specializing in moral and political philosophy and the philosophy of law, Esquith is author of articles on Rawls, Marx, Weber, Emerson, and such topics in democratic theory as the rule of law, transitional justice, and political education. He is author of *Intimacy and Spectacle: Liberal Theory as Political Education* (1994), editor of *Political Dialogue: Theories and Practices* (1996), and author of *The Political Responsibilities of Everyday Bystanders* (forthcoming).

William A. Galston is senior fellow in governance studies at the Brookings Institution. He is a political theorist who both studies and participates in American politics and domestic policy. Galston was deputy assistant to the president for domestic policy during the first Clinton Administration (1993–1995) and executive director of the National Commission on Civic Renewal (1996–1998). He has served as director of Economic and Social Programs at the Roosevelt Center for American Policy Studies in Washington, D.C., as chief speech writer for John Anderson's National Unity campaign, as issues director for Walter Mondale's presidential campaign, and as senior advisor to Albert Gore Jr. during his run for the Democratic presidential nomination in 1988 and the presidency in 2000. Since 1995, Galston has served as a founding member of the Board of the National Campaign to Prevent Teen Pregnancy and as chair of the campaign's Task Force on Religion and Public Values. He is author of more than one hundred articles and of eight books, the most recent of which are *Liberal Pluralism* (2002), *The Practice of Liberal Pluralism* (2004), and *Public Matters: Politics, Policy, and Religion in the 21st Century* (2005).

Verna V. Gehring is editor at the Institute for Philosophy and Public Policy at the School of Public Policy, University of Maryland. She is a philosopher broadly interested in the obligations of state and citizen and the various accounts of civil society. In addition to her work on the seventeenth-century political philosopher Thomas Hobbes and his enduring influence, Gehring's interest is applied to such contemporary matters as the state lottery, nuclear proliferation, computer hackers, baseball scandals, and the social harms caused by imposters. Gehring teaches in the graduate program at the School of Public Policy. She is author of several articles, editor in chief of *Philosophy & Public Policy Quarterly*, coeditor (with William A. Galston) of *Philosophical Dimensions of Public Policy* (2002), and editor of *War after September 11* (2002), *Genetic Prospects: Essays on Biotechnology, Ethics, and Public Policy* (2003), *The Internet in Public Life* (2004), and *Community Matters: Challenges to Civic Engagement in the 21st Century* (2005).

Xiaorong Li is research scholar at the Institute for Philosophy and Public Policy, School for Public Policy, at the University of Maryland. She has written articles on human rights, culture, reproductive rights, and gender issues. She is the author of *Ethics, Human Rights, and Culture* (2006).

Roland Pierik is assistant professor in political theory, Department of Political Science, Nijmegen University, the Netherlands. His current research interest is contemporary political theory, especially liberal egalitarianism in plural and multicultural societies, and issues of global justice. He is the author of numerous papers, including "Slavery Reparations and Distributive Justice," *Journal of Social Philosophy* (2006) and "Western Policies on Child Labor Abroad," *Ethics & International Affairs* (2006; coauthored with Mijke Houwerzijl), and "Resources versus Capabilities: Social Endowments in Egalitarian Theory," *Political Studies*, (forthcoming; coauthored with Ingrid Robeyns).